Bing Thom

Bing Thom Works

Princeton Architectural Press, New York

Published by
Princeton Architectural Press
37 East Seventh Street
New York, New York 10003

For a free catalog of books, call 1.800.722.6657.
Visit our website at www.papress.com.

Printed and bound in China
14 13 12 11 4 3 2 1 First edition

Editor: Dan Simon
Designer: Jan Haux

Special thanks to: Bree Anne Apperley, Sara Bader, Nicola Bednarek Brower, Janet Behning, Megan Carey, Carina Cha, Tom Cho, Penny (Yuen Pik) Chu, Russell Fernandez, Pete Fitzpatrick, Linda Lee, John Myers, Katharine Myers, Andrew Stepanian, Jennifer Thompson, Paul Wagner, Joseph Weston, and Deb Wood of Princeton Architectural Press —Kevin C. Lippert, publisher

Library of Congress Cataloging-in-Publication Data
Bing Thom Architects.
Bing Thom works / Bing Thom Architects. — 1st ed.
p. cm.
ISBN 978-1-56898-959-4 (alk. paper)
1. Bing Thom Architects. 2. Architecture, Modern—20th century.
3. Architecture, Modern—21st century. I. Title.
NA737.B52A4 2010
720.92'2—dc22

2010007053

Contents

Foreword

by Fumihiko Maki

As the author himself states, this is not the typical architect's monograph. Within, Bing Thom has selected a number of projects from the many works and proposals produced in his thirty-year career and through them explains to the reader the questions he has spent his life asking. What is architecture? What is the right approach to architectural design?

Over the years I have known Thom, I have come to see that we are alike in that we have both continued to live and practice in the city in which we were raised and educated, Vancouver in his case and Tokyo in mine. I believe hometowns make the most desirable base of operation for architects. That is because experiences with their hometowns offer the best, and often times the only, opportunities for architects to think about the basic nature of human beings and communities. Certainly there are as many different hometowns and human relationships as there are architects, but as contradictory as it may seem, we can gain an understanding of the universality of human nature only through experiences in the societies to which we individually commit ourselves. I myself have been involved in many projects in Tokyo over the last fifty years, but I believe I would not have been able to get in touch with the essence of its contemporary community had I not been involved with a project that lasted for forty years, as I was with Hillside Terrace.

The essay entitled "Vancouver" in this book vividly describes Thom's love of the city and his participation on many different levels in the development of this region. On the eternal question of the relationship between architect and client, he emphasizes the importance of mutual understanding and trust between the two parties. In his redevelopment projects, dialogues with local governments, developers, diverse user groups, and residents were no doubt necessary, making it clear that such dialogue gives birth to new design-planning themes. Examples of works outside the Vancouver region introduced in this book include Arena Stage in Washington, D.C., and Tarrant County College in Fort Worth, Texas. The former is a case where he has made use on a conceptual level of his experience jumpstarting neighborhood transformation in Vancouver. In Fort Worth, his community college also provides flood control, not by simple embankment work, but by the construction of a new bypass channel intended to revitalize a district adjoining downtown. Thus his concern for the long-term needs of communities in Vancouver has been transferred to, and found expression in, places far from Canada.

Another item on his agenda is assuring quality in buildings, whatever their type. Around the time he opened his office in the early 1980s, Vancouver's economy had hit rock bottom. In the process of working on a small apartment building, a warehouse, and a design office for himself, he gained experience as a master builder. He explains how he was able to learn the importance of controlling the budget and schedule from architectural design to completion and collaborating with people of different professions during that process. He goes on to describe the passionate pursuit of his ultimate objective, which is the creation of high-quality buildings.

He also points out that in order to assure architectural quality, collaboration with trustworthy craftsmen under the architect's leadership in critical aspects of design is indispensable. By craftsmen, he means not just artisans in the traditional sense but also subcontractors and fabricators dealing with new materials such as glass, metals, and wood. The Chan Centre for the Performing Arts impressed me as a building that reaches a high degree of perfection. It is an elegant composition of forms set in a forest that, inside, skillfully meets the complex functional demands of a concert hall. Having learned from this book how it is a crystallization of his holistic approach, I am struck once more by admiration for his achievement.

*The Craftsman**, a much-discussed book by sociologist Richard Sennett, defines craftsman quite broadly, including as a computer programmer, for example, and takes craftsmanship today to mean "the basic human impulse to do a job well for its own sake." As Thom points out, architecture is rapidly undergoing commodification amid globalization, and there is, at times, a tendency among both architects and the media to glorify novelty even when devoid of content. However, as Sennett's book suggests, objections to that tendency are also increasingly being raised around the world. The fact that, at such a time, one architect based in Vancouver has put together a volume detailing his convictions and the results of his efforts to create buildings of high quality is extremely timely and meaningful.

*Richard Sennett, *The Craftsman* (New Haven, CT: Yale University Press, 2008).

Preface

If you live in a city in North America, chances are you spend 50 to 90 percent of your life inside buildings. That is a staggering statistic, and proves why good architecture is so important. We need good buildings to nourish us, just like food or fresh air or sunlight.

Translating our ideas and work into a book is a challenging experience. As architects, we communicate in a three-dimensional language. Translating architecture into static text and graphics can never explain the work; a building must be *experienced.* A book may capture aspects of the feeling or mood of a building, but it is only through movement, touch, sound, light, and space that a building is brought to life. A book can be a literary or visual work of art but it can never be architecture.

So why this book, now? We believe that we are in a period where many question the value of architecture. We have recently witnessed an age of architectural exuberance that mutated into an age of excess. Architecture became a commodity; people and cities believed a designer-branded building could somehow reinvent them for the better. Our hope is that this book may speak to those who are just beginning their architectural careers and those who want to reflect on what architecture is really about. Architecture is more than art. We have a social responsibility as architects; we affect people's lives; and we *can* change the nature of our society, but only after digging deep and asking tough questions. With the majority of the world's population now living in cities, the possibilities—and urgent need—have never been greater for this planet.

We don't mean this book to be a monograph. The three-section format is non-linear. We begin the book with where we *are* today rather than rationalize how we got there—Arena Stage in Washington, D.C., our most recent major project. Like other projects in parts of cities that many people would rather forget, Arena is changing the neighborhood. These "edge" projects are what we now find most exciting and meaningful; and it is here that the world can change for the better. How do you regenerate wasted space, whether it's in the middle of a city or on the edge? Some would describe our focus as regenerative urbanism. We just know that our greatest desire is to give people a deeper sense of community. If there are barriers, we want to break them down. Meaningful buildings can do that.

You'll find a series of essays in the middle of this book that illustrate our creative process. It's a philosophical and practical process we have developed that supports our own wish to practice the craft of architecture in its infinite scale, from designing handrails to entire cities. We've described it all in a way intended to make you feel part of a conversation. If you can't physically experience our buildings, you can at least join us behind-the-scenes of seven very different projects described in the book's last section.

In the end, each building is judged long after the opening ceremony and the photo essays. Does the building have depth? Poetry? Does it capture spiritual values *and* satisfy more utilitarian needs? Can the building withstand the test of time? Have we made a difference? Did the building deserve to be built?

Bing Thom and Michael Heeney, October 2010

Arena Stage

The Project

When Molly Smith, Arena Stage's creative director, told us the theater company's mission statement is to serve all that is "passionate, exuberant, profound, deep, and dangerous in the American spirit," we thought, "dangerous—that's for us!"

Arena Stage was Washington, D.C.'s first major resident acting company. Always at the vanguard, Arena is recognized as one of America's finest regional theaters, and a pioneer in many ways. It was the first to integrate its audiences; the first to make theater accessible to people with disabilities, including sign interpretation and audio description; and the first regional theater to transfer a production to Broadway: *The Great White Hope* debuted in New York's Alvin Theater in 1968 with Arena's original cast that included a young, then-unknown actor named James Earl Jones. Even Arena's original Fichandler Stage rates as an architectural footnote. Designed in 1960 by the great Chicago modernist Harry Weese (also architect of Washington's stunning Metro stations), the Fichandler was one of the first theaters-in-the-round built in modern times. So when the board said they wanted to abandon Arena's two heritage buildings (including the Kreeger Stage, added in 1971) and relocate, we urged them not to run away from Arena's history. True, Arena was in Southwest Washington, in a neighborhood that had never recovered from the destruction associated with a brutal urban renewal attempt in the 1960s, but we were convinced we *should* reinvent Arena, that we could create something extraordinary on the original site, and that we could use Arena as a catalyst to reinvigorate the neighborhood.

Our approach was inspired by the three temples on the Acropolis. The Fichandler Stage and Kreeger Theater themselves were largely untouched, but we demolished the theaters' connecting structures, including lobbies and offices, burying all the back-of-house administration and classrooms. We added the Kogod Cradle Theater, and celebrated the three—two heritage, one new—by wrapping them in glass, topped by a lavish roof that just happens to be on axis with the Washington Monument. It is a salute to the new America.

In terms of space, they wanted us to double the size of their facilities on the same site. Molly wanted the two existing theaters to be refurbished, and to attract specific audiences: the Fichandler would feature classic American plays, the Kreeger would present contemporary American theater. The new 200-seat Cradle Theater would nurture emerging plays and voices from throughout America. Most important was a lobby large enough to allow audiences to mingle during intermissions and at the end of performances. She wanted different audiences to collide and share their Arena experiences. An architect can only be as good as the client allows you to be. Molly Smith was willing to go right to the edge with us.

The lobby is large enough to accommodate the audiences of all three venues at the same time, allowing them the opportunity to collide and share their experiences. It is really composed of a series of "found" spaces between, around, and on top of the theaters. As a result you can never see the whole space and you are constantly tantalized and intrigued by what might be around the corner. This natural desire to investigate the space is further heightened by providing multiple opportunities to people watch—allowing the audience to be either actor or voyeur as they explore.

ARENA STAGE AT TH

ENTER FOR AMERIC THEATER

The New Container

The neighborhood has become much noisier since the Fichlander was constructed in the early 1960s. Air traffic from nearby Reagan National Airport had radically increased and it was common to have shows interrupted by noise from sirens. So as a result, one of the key technical requirements we faced in renovating the two existing theaters was to improve their acoustic isolation from outside noise. This was complicated significantly by the fact that the theaters are listed as historic structures and Washington is a city that takes historic structures more seriously than most. As a result, there is not much you can physically alter. To get around this dilemma, we came up with the idea of wrapping the theaters in a transparent building skin that would keep the noise out. This ended up taking the form of a 55-foot-high laminated glass wall surrounding the buildings. This also enclosed the space between the theaters, creating the large lobby that Molly was keen on.

Although our first interest was to use the glass wall to provide acoustic isolation from sirens and aircraft, we also wanted to maximize transparency. We wanted people passing by to see the activity inside, as well as theatergoers to see out, because there is a great view of the Washington Channel.

In order to maximize the wall's transparency we tilted the glass to minimize reflections, similar to an aircraft control tower. These big, high, tilted glass windows were an idea that originated in the Chan Centre for the Performing Arts. We experimented with them again on Surrey's Central City—they were even taller there, but still remained tilted to minimize the reflection. To accomplish that feat in Surrey we introduced a wooden support system. These are large, heavy timber columns that

do double duty. They hold up the roof *and* they hold up the glass/window system. Traditionally, window system structures are completely independent from the structure that supports the roof, but by sharing the roof and window structure it drives down structural costs and allows you to do something special.

Although conceptually similar to Central City (see p. 104), we wanted the Arena building to be even more transparent, so we spaced Arena's columns farther apart, allowing us to use bigger sheets of glass. To support this, the columns had to grow in size, but we shaped them into an elliptical form to reduce their visual impact.

The big challenge with timber construction is the connections. In particular, we wanted to celebrate how the columns meet the ground. For Central City, we developed a design for a ductile iron casting that was hinged to accommodate the sloped glass wall. We could have just reused the base supports we designed for Surrey. But we said, "No, let's design a new support." These new bases for the Arena columns recall the delicacy of a ballet dancer *en pointe*.

Although we had done it before in Surrey, no one had ever used timber construction for a large commercial building in Washington. We needed to get special permission and convince the authorities that building with wood is safe. As a result, this is the first heavy timber project in Washington. We received approval during a very long and drawn out lumber trade dispute between Canada and the United States, and the Canadian ambassador joked that we had more success dealing with the issue in a few short months than he had over several years. In order to build this system, we brought in the same craftsmen we had used in Surrey to manufacture and install these huge columns.

AREN
STAG

ER FOR AMERICAN THEATER

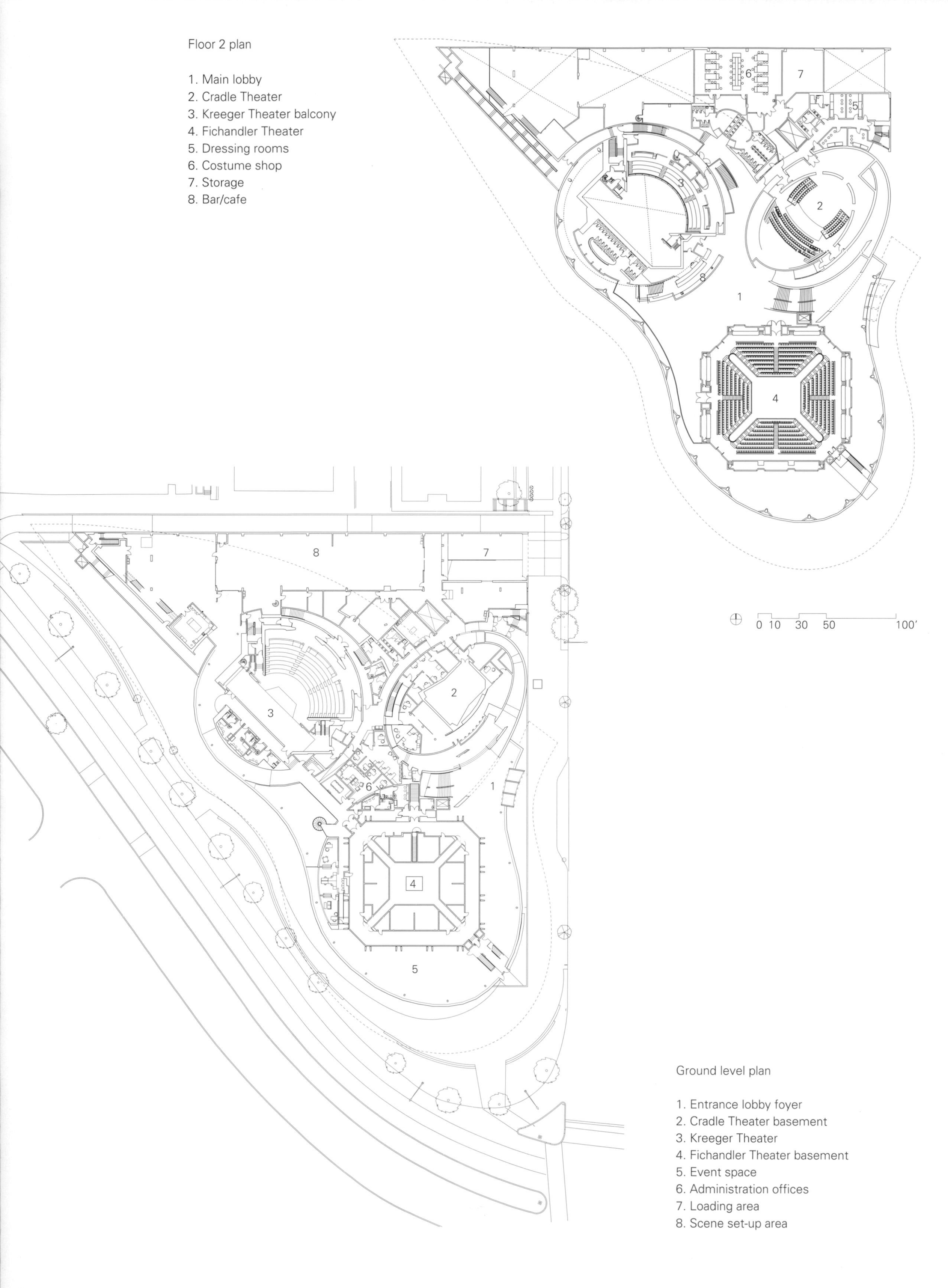
Floor 2 plan
1. Main lobby
2. Cradle Theater
3. Kreeger Theater balcony
4. Fichandler Theater
5. Dressing rooms
6. Costume shop
7. Storage
8. Bar/cafe
0 10 30 50 100'
Ground level plan
1. Entrance lobby foyer
2. Cradle Theater basement
3. Kreeger Theater
4. Fichandler Theater basement
5. Event space
6. Administration offices
7. Loading area
8. Scene set-up area

CONCESSIONS

FICHANDLER STAGE

The Arlene and Robert Kogod Cradle Theater

Christened "the Cradle" by Molly, this new theater is meant to support the creation of new plays and cradle risk. Because the Cradle was meant to nurture new plays, we wanted an oval shape that had some character of its own, to let the artists feel safe and comfortable taking risks.

However, the oval shape is very bad for acoustics; concave walls focus sound to different parts of the interior space, making it harder to hear. Our two objectives were working against each other. We needed an acoustically permeable wall that was also visually enveloping. First we tried to do it using a series of telephone poles to contain the space. They were vertical, and had gaps where the sound could go through. The verticality and scale of the poles did not feel quite right, so we changed tack and looked at a horizontal arrangement of wooden boards. We spaced the boards so that sound would leak through the gaps, to offset the focusing tendencies of the curve. We built a full scale mock-up in our parking lot and the acousticians came up from Chicago to test it. The mock-up failed: The sound still had some undesirable focusing issues. We really liked the horizontal appearance, we just needed to find a way to disperse the sound while generally maintaining the same visual style. Finally, we came up with the idea of weaving the wood like a basket. This sounded good in theory, but we were immediately asked how we could practically achieve this. Again, we got back to building a mock-up. This time we brought in a shipwright who taught us how to steam wood, making it pliable enough to take the basket weave curves, and the acoustics worked!

Aside from the acoustics of the theater itself, the Cradle presented us with another challenge. People entering the theater would be moving from a large lobby, able to easily accommodate 1,400 people, into an intimate 200-seat space. This change of scale is quite profound and we did not want it to be too abrupt. Transitions

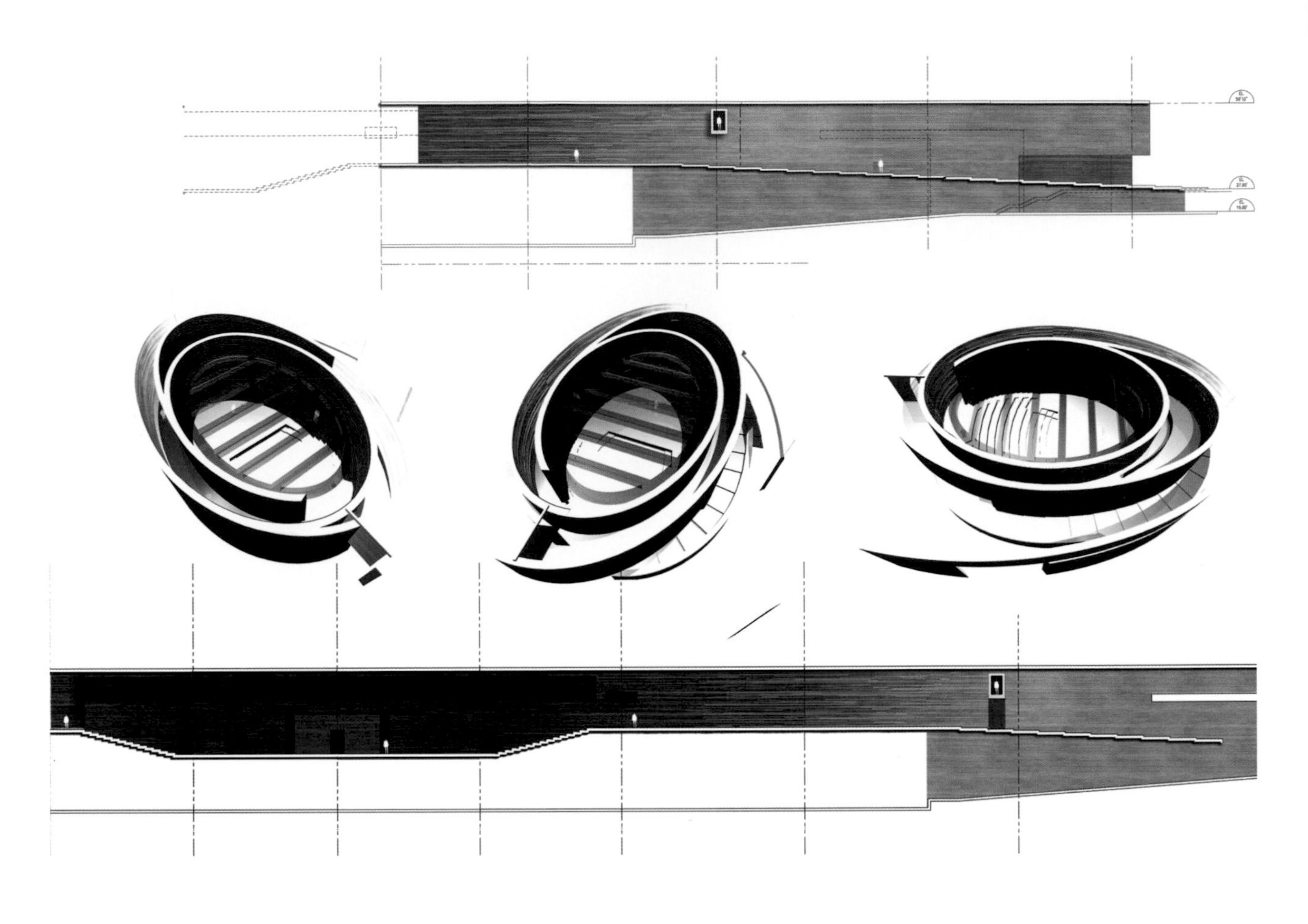

are very important. In fact, designing good architectural transitions is sometimes more important than designing the spaces, because the transition sets up the room's experience. From a technical standpoint we also needed to create a sound- and light-lock between the lobby and the Cradle Theater. Our solution was inspired by Richard Serra's elliptical steel sculptures. We separated the lobby's sound and light from the theater's by bringing the audience in through a narrow spiral entry. Journeying into the Cradle, you lose the memory of the big space you have just left. By "squeezing" people we gave them a unique experience, one that introduced the drama of a new space. So, when they actually enter the small theater, it seems to be quite a large space in comparison.

Originally we had planned to build the Cradle with steel construction because that seemed to be the lightest and simplest way to do it. But because the exterior of the spiral shape was to be clad with zinc and the interior with wood, there would be this very complicated material transition. In the end, with the help and advice of the contractor, we switched to concrete, which is much more coherent and (to the delight of all) less expensive. We left the concrete exposed. Now the Cradle is much stronger as a building than it would have been had it been built on a steel frame. It is a very powerful form—for the audience, it will be a powerful experience.

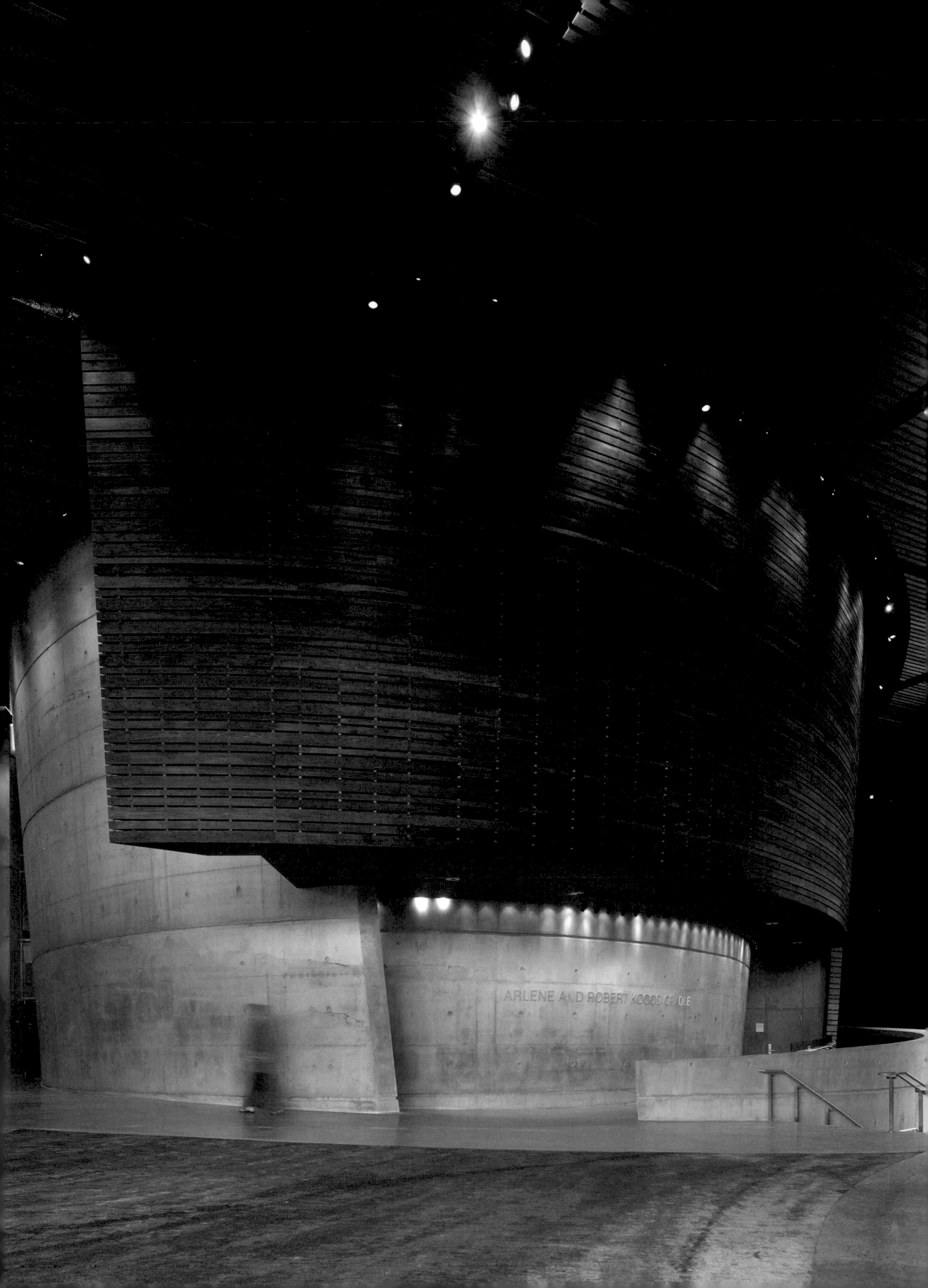
ARLENE AND ROBERT KOGOD CRADLE

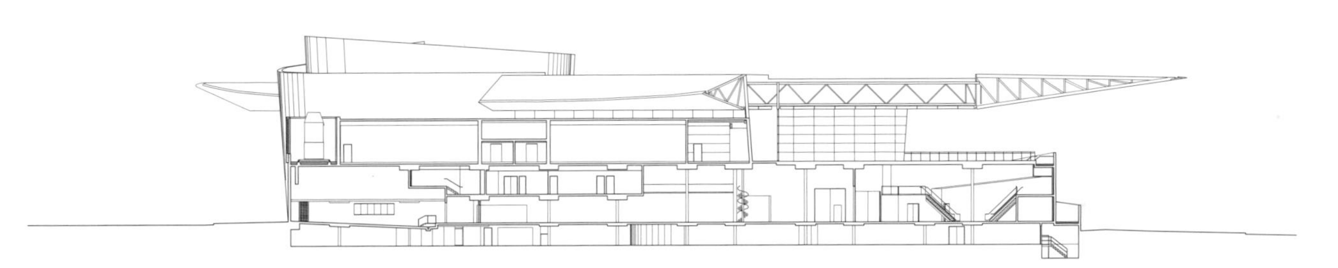

Longitudinal section 2

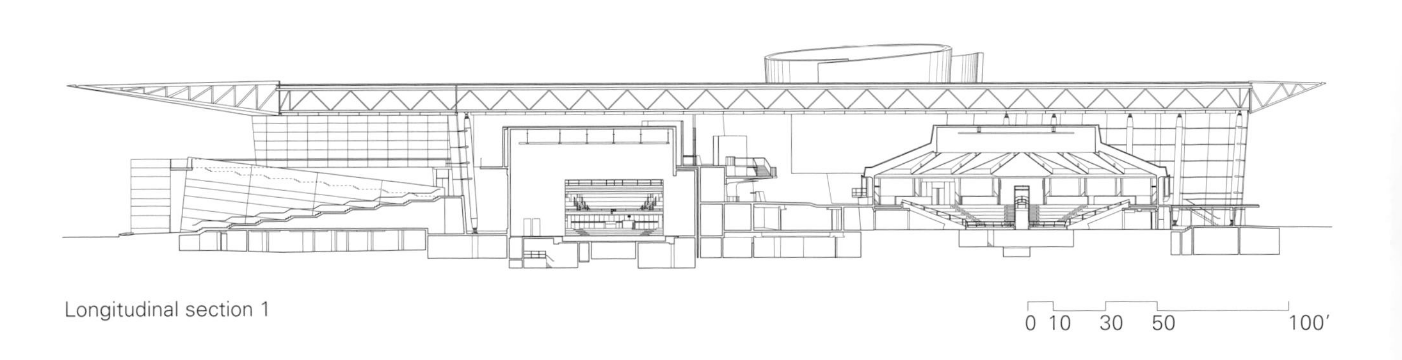

Longitudinal section 1

0 10 30 50 100′

Southeastern
University

Master Builder

It is easy to forget that architecture as a profession is only 150 years old; we prefer a traditional practice that looks back to the way of the master builders. Before the Industrial Revolution there were no architects, just master builders like Michelangelo and Andrea Palladio during the Italian Renaissance, or John Nash in London's Regency period. These men did not separate the roles of development, design, and construction. It was all one thing, and they built beautiful buildings and designed cities that made people proud.

As master builders, they took responsibility for each project, and in return they held creative authority. That was the vision behind Bing Thom Architects when we started in 1981. The early 1980s were a terrible time in Vancouver's economy—interest rates were at almost 20 percent and there were no clients. So we became our own client and built our office, tucked under Burrard Bridge. We were developer, architect, and contractor all in one. In fact, it was our first design-build experience.

Six of us physically put the building up during a city-wide strike, while Vancouver's permit department was closed. By the time the department got back to work and issued a stop work order, we had finished. Because we did not have any drawings, we made changes as we went. When we first put up the walls and the ceiling looked too low, we said, "Let's go higher," and we dropped the walls, added about four feet, put it all back up, and said, "Yeah, that feels about right." That is how master builders have always worked: by experimenting. We had begun to learn the whole craft of producing buildings, working out of a trailer parked on site as Bing Thom Architects's first office. It has been a journey that started with small family projects, like a relative's warehouse and an apartment building where one of us has a unit.

During Vancouver's EXPO 86 the pace picked up and we received commissions for several pavilions,

including one for Hong Kong, for which we were responsible for designing and building. By the late 1980s, the majority of projects in the office were on our own account. We had created a sister company called ARDEC (short for ARchitecture, DEsign, and Construction) that put together real estate deals. We would find a real estate opportunity, design the project, assemble a consortium of investors, build the project, and sell it. This allowed us, a relatively young and modest-sized practice, to work on interesting projects with a fantastic client: ourselves.

We built one of the first large mixed-use projects in Vancouver when we stacked a slim condominium tower on top of a custom office for a large pulp and paper engineering firm. Our chance to do something beyond the standard "spec" office building came with another Vancouver project, adjacent the Provincial Law Courts—the same law courts for which Bing Thom was project architect when he worked with Arthur Erickson in the 1970s. We started that project by negotiating a deal with the city government which granted us development concessions and allowed us to include independent space for a local non-profit arts group. We also collaborated with a sculptor to develop a unique, cloud-inspired canopy on the same building. Both were ideas that most bottom-line developers would not even consider. Throughout all of this we were learning first-hand about both the importance and the advantages of being involved in all aspects of a project—of being master builders. We discovered that creativity is not limited to design. If a project can be managed creatively, it will in turn create all kinds of opportunities for great architecture to occur.

Why Risk?

After we won the design competition and Hong Kong's client consortium hired us to design their pavilion for EXPO 86, the client said we expect you to not only *design* our building, but we want you to get it constructed, and tell us how to operate it during the six-month world exposition. "Here's seven million dollars. If there's any left over, keep it. But if you run out, don't come back to us." In our firm's early days that risk was scary, but it forced us into new areas and gave us the opportunity to work in partnership with people we liked and trusted. Most important, it gave us artistic freedom.

If architects want control—and architects *do* want it, because control is just another word for artistic freedom—then we have to take responsibility. You cannot have one without the other, and with responsibility comes risk.

That has been a problem in our profession. We routinely take on other enormous risks, gravity for instance. We don't think twice about being legally responsible for making sure a building does not fall down; yet architects throw up their hands and say, "We're not prepared to take responsibility for costs."

What we are saying is, if architects are afraid of risk—the risk of liabilities, risk of failure, risk of going over budget—then you are forever narrowing your field of effect. You have to say to the client, "Don't worry—*we* will be responsible, but we must have the creative authority to go with it." Then you can control the budget, control the schedule and the quality, *and* you can maintain artistic control. You must be responsible, of course, and not be foolish enough to go bankrupt, but you have to be willing to take that risk. The more you get marginalized to just one aspect of a project, the more difficult it is to deal with risk. Result? You become more conservative and do lousy buildings because you cannot control the risk. But when you broaden your involvement, risk is easier to manage.

Consider two scenarios: In the first, you are hired as the architect and given a budget. You are aware that if you go over budget, that is a huge risk. You are very cautious. In the second scenario, you say, "I'm going to be involved in everything. I've got a great idea, and yes, it costs more than the budget allows, but if I have the ability to redistribute the budget or to go out and find the money to pay for that idea, then I've offset that risk."

The Chan Centre for the Performing Arts is a great example. We inherited a budget that was so low that it was considered pure science fiction by concert hall experts. Before we were even hired, the university was in the awkward position of having promised their major patron an elaborate performing arts center for their donation. By the time a knowledgeable theater-cost consultant advised them of the true cost, it was too late to renege on the commitment, so we were in a very sticky spot. But Chan's very tight budget forced us to prioritize, to figure out what was important and how still to make the building work.

We wanted to clad the exterior in zinc, something we had successfully pioneered for the Canada Pavilion at Spain's Expo '92, so we found a donor to pay for that. Because there was no money available for the fine interior finishes typically associated with these facilities, we spent a tremendous amount of time detailing the concrete and steel structure so that it was attractive in its own right and could be left exposed. Similarly, we had no landscape budget, so we had to improvise. We tagged, dug out, and stored over two hundred rhododendrons and azaleas that were growing on the site so that we could replant them after construction. This resulted in a fantastic, mature landscape; probably better than we could have done if we had the budget to purchase new planting.

In the end, it's not about money: Architecture is about passion. *Then* you make the money work, but you don't start with it. We're not out there to go broke; we are realistic enough about money that we know what it takes. But first you have got to have that sense that you are in it to create a work of art that will change people's lives. Then risk that you can do it.

On Risk

A Close Collaboration with Trusted Craftsmen

We hope clients are drawn to us because we are willing to push the envelope and to try something new. In fact, we often say that if a client already knows what kind of building they want, we are probably not the right architects for them. When both client and architect agree to focus on pushing that envelope, as architects we must be responsible and have a method of working that can control the technical and cost risks that are inevitably involved. The key is to reduce financial risk while maximizing the opportunity for innovation. Here is how we try to do it at BTA.

Traditionally, clients hire an architect and then a contractor, with the architect administering the construction contract. Increasingly, in these strained economic times, clients simply hire a contractor and leave it to them to hire the architect and look after the design. What this means is that the architect no longer has a direct connection with the client. This kind of design-build is a recipe for mediocre and unsatisfying work. Our firm routinely turns down this sort of design-build project because it constricts creativity. Instead, we have redefined design-build to put ourselves back into equal partnership with the client and the general contractor.

What is different? We still maintain the traditional role of the general contractor, but we initially keep major building components out of that contract so that we can get an opportunity to work directly with the skilled craftsmen whom we trust to produce these critical building components. We feel that most general contractors, when they bid on a project, as soon as they spot components that are unusual, or maybe just something they have not done before, they allocate a whole lot of "risk" money against these items in their bid. The tragedy is that very often it's these unusual, innovative elements that give the architecture its character. When they are lost, the negative impact on the design can be profound. More often than not there is absolutely no rational basis for this; typically the general contractor does not understand what is being asked, or he does not have the time and resources to try and understand. This all-too-frequent scenario jeopardizes these components of a project, or results in cutting them out all together because of costs. You as client or contractor do not have the time or inclination to understand and take the risk? Fine. We'll put together a team who will.

Prior to going out to tender, when we are still refining a detailed design, we find "craftsmen," which is what we prefer to call those sub-contractors whom we trust, and who trust us, to design-build the feature in question for a specific amount of money. Together with the client, we agree on a fixed price, and that amount is then carried in the construction budget. Working closely with these craftsmen, we refine the design to meet the budget, and once that is settled the contract is then assigned to the general contractor. This way, the general contractor does not put any risk money against these items. We take on the risk, but this risk is mitigated because we are working with tradesmen whom we trust, collaborate with, and know that together we will work within the budget. Result? The client's budget is protected and so is our design—everyone wins.

Almost all of our significant projects have used this method. In the case of the Chan Centre for the Performing Arts, we had two unique elements to deal with. One was a 37-ton adjustable acoustic canopy for the concert hall, the other was a series of portable three-story seating towers for the studio theater. We pulled both of these out of the general construction contract and then re-assigned them once we had worked out all the details. On a smaller scale, when we wanted to do something extraordinary for the women's washroom but were really counting pennies, we took a slightly different approach: we commissioned a young architect who had worked in our office as a student to design and build it. This washroom never stops getting accolades. It has been featured in several movies and TV series, including a *Battlestar Galactica* episode.

With Aberdeen Centre, where we wanted the exterior cladding of this urban shopping mall to be a

dynamic work of art, we took on the all-glass exterior as a separate design-build. Although the innovative wall, a translucent gel film sandwiched between glass, was initially more expensive than stucco, we were able to convince our client that it was more cost effective for the project as a whole. By prefabricating the glass walls off-site he could bring in tenants—and rent—one month sooner than if we used stucco.

For the three extensive heavy timber components we used in Surrey Central City, we entered into our largest design-build subcontract yet. In this case we used a firm that was established by one of our structural engineering consultants, back when we were working on the Pacific Canada Pavilion for the Vancouver Aquarium. We needed to design a long span structure to go over one of the exhibits. We chose to design it out of timber because a steel structure would have been damaged by the corrosive salt water in the exhibit. We spent an inordinate amount of time detailing these beautiful stainless steel and wood trusses, but when the bids came in, the trusses were way over budget. Our structural engineer said, "This is a ridiculous price, I'll build them myself for the original budget," and so a new company was born. We have probably worked on half a dozen different projects with them since then.

Our version of design-build works because the best craftsmen and craftswomen enter the trades because they love the work and seek out challenges. These people often comes to us with ways of solving these design challenges that we had never considered. It is truly give and take. We don't separate the creative process from what is in the office and what is in the field. That's what is wonderful about design-build. We are able to incorporate the experience of contractors to make the architecture even better.

Who Says Money and Art Are Polar Opposites?

There is an aura about architecture, reinforced by Ayn Rand's *The Fountainhead* (1943), that money and art are polar opposites. They are not. Picasso and Andy Warhol were great businessmen, so was Michelangelo. Yet in architecture school, money is never talked about as being part of the balance: it is talked about as the cause of compromise. You do not find that attitude in Chinese culture, for example, where our firm has done a number of projects over the past two decades. When you hire an architect in China, discussion about money is just a natural part of it.

Regardless of where you're building, money spent on additional "up front" design time can pay off handsomely. When we were working on one of our own early Vancouver development projects, a twenty-six-story large mixed-use building, we designed a canopy around the outside of the building. After talking to one of the steel fabricators, who had new and very efficient cutting equipment, we were able to design the whole canopy so that there would be no waste. Even though we needed unusual angles, every piece of steel that we cut was done in such a way that both halves could be used. We had to spend an extra ten thousand dollars on design time, but we saved over one hundred thousand dollars in material.

Collaborating with trades also means we use traditional construction in new ways. With Sunset Community Centre, we saved up to a month and a half of construction time and considerable cost by using a standard warehouse construction technique called concrete tilt-up. It's a very fast way to build, and very inexpensive. The big difference was that instead of using the tilt-up walls on the exterior, as they do with warehouses, we used them for the principal interior walls. We discovered that we could get a fantastic and highly

durable marble-like finish on the concrete. It required extra design and supervision time to make sure that all the exposed components and services in the walls were correctly located, but the results were stunning.

The trick is to come as close as possible to the absolute budget. Regardless of how we do it, we want to maximize the value in every project. Everyone is terrified of going over budget, but we think it's just as bad to come in under budget. Conservative architects and clients will say, "We'll just design to 80 percent of the budget and we'll keep 20 percent in our pocket as backup that we can add in later." But even if you decide to add in that 20 percent later, you will only get a fraction of the value. If you want to get the most value, you have to be really aggressive with the budget.

Compromise Is Not in Our Vocabulary—Balance Is

You could say "compromise" is not in our vocabulary. Compromise has too negative a connotation. We think of "balance," not compromise. As a master builder, you take the responsibility to create the balance in every project. Our design process is to find the right balance between budget, time, aesthetics, function, human need, and culture. Again, it comes back to the architect having that control or creative freedom. It lets you control priorities as you adjust that balance. When we had to cut 20 percent of the budget for Arena Stage, we were forced to redesign the roof. Redesign became refinement. Many aspects of Arena's new roof are better because of it.

And when we say "balance," we don't mean a state of static balance. That balance is constantly evolving, constantly in a spiral, constantly moving. Balance is another way of explaining "master builder." It's a different way of asking, "How do you practice architecture? How do you create beautiful, meaningful things in our society?"

Commodification of Architecture Is Going Global

Many architects have become shoppers. They don't design anymore. Rather than come up with something original, all too often architects just go into the catalogs and shop for window systems, shop for doors, for flooring, sinks...whatever; each is a package deal. The architects knit all these packages together, and that's the building. That's why so much architecture in North America looks the same. It's all from the same catalogs, and this trend is getting worse. It's not just a North American disease; catalog shopping is happening globally. It is the opposite of our master builder philosophy. Similarly, some architects prefer to just design the building and then hand it off to another firm for the construction drawings. We are loath to do that. What clients do not understand is that the second architect, who isn't the designer, is only thinking about his or her own liability and profit margin. So that person wants to do the drawings in the cheapest and safest way possible, which usually means something out of a catalog.

It all comes back to economics: money. If you are only paid a set fee and you have only so many hours, you're going to maximize what you can do, so you shop instead of doing the detailing yourself. As long as it has the right look and brand recognition, it doesn't matter that you're just shopping, or riding on someone else's design. You protect your fee and you do not risk lawsuits, but is it architecture? For Calgary's SAIT Polytechnic project, we had to cover the wall of an enormous parking garage—the length of a football field—with a screen. We could have flipped through a catalog and chosen a grille. Instead, we decided to work with an artist to develop a screen with differently angled perforations that behave like pixels creating a photographic image. True, what we

propose means more time on our part, more sweat goes into it, but the physical building is not more expensive.

Architecture has become a commodity. Developers brand their projects with architects' names to increase their profit. The purchaser is not buying that condominium as a home; he or she is buying it as a branded investment. They're not looking at the quality of the creativity as in, "Is this a place I want to live in?" Rather, "Is it a place I can eventually sell to someone else?" We are keenly interested in that personal relationship between ourselves and the end user. As a result, now we do very little work for run-of-the-mill developers. They don't see the value. They try to push down the price for everything. All the creative decisions are made by the client, not the architect.

We are fortunate enough now to work only with clients who want to collaborate, who appreciate craftsmanship, and who are willing to take risks. One of our first design-build projects was the Northwest Territories (NWT) pavilion at EXPO 86. When the client first came to us, they said they only had enough money to decorate six prefab-construction trailers. We said, no, no—give us the same budget and we'll design a building for you. The glittering iceberg-inspired NWT pavilion of painted plywood and fine glass granules was voted one of EXPO's top five most popular pavilions by visitors and the international press, despite having one of the smallest budgets.

Vancouver Effect

Our thinking has been profoundly influenced by where we live.

We believe that because of Vancouver's location, people, geography, and relative youth, it is a place where work can be done differently. For example, once we had a highly respected glass consultant come from New York to Vancouver to help us with the curtain wall system for Surrey Central City. At the end of our meeting, we asked if we could pick his brain about a glass sculpture we wanted to do for a small, private house commission. We talked about it for a while, but soon realized that we needed to get advice from someone who might actually help us build it. Vancouver has a number of glass artists and craftsmen, so we picked up the phone and called one saying, "I've got a consultant here; can you come down in forty-five minutes to talk about this?" When he arrived, we explained what we were trying to do and asked if he was interested. He said yes. We asked, "Can we have a sample next week?" He said yes. After he left, the glass consultant said, "This is incredible: You phone this person, you ask him to come in forty-five minutes, you ask him to do something he's never done before in his life, and you ask him for a sample next week. You could never do that in New York, in Los Angeles, or London. If you ask someone to do something they've never done before, they're not interested. They don't have time, and they worry that they're not going to make enough money."

The consultant's amazement confirmed what we suspected: living in Vancouver gives us an advantage. It's not because everybody here is from somewhere else. It's because you run away to Vancouver if you don't want to be in New York, or Los Angeles, or London. Result? We've got a collection of craftsmen, both builders and artists, who are here in Vancouver because they want to live their lives in a certain way. Recently, for example, we discovered some Russian tile setters working on Aberdeen Centre who came to Vancouver by way of Italy, where they were restoring the Sistine Chapel. These people are not just motivated by making money; they take on unusual projects because they're a challenge, and because they will enrich their lives in other ways. Like us, they want to do impossible projects if they will make

a difference. These mutual interests and goals are the basis of a trust that makes it possible for us to do the work that we do.

Vancouverites are edge people, and Vancouver—founded in 1886, burned to the ground in 1887—is on the edge of the continent, equidistant from both Europe and Asia. But, really, it is Asia, not Europe, that has most strongly affected BTA's conception of space in architecture, where the negative is as important as the positive. The way we design our buildings, the whole idea is open plan, open flow. We don't think of walls and structures, we think of free circulation and rhythms. There is no concept of outside and inside, no separation between man and nature; there is no emphasis on where the front is (sometimes there is no difference between the front door and the back door), and there is not that much difference between the window and the door. Even our concept of the "skin" of the building is very permeable, often glass or screens.

Vancouver has been called an Asian city located in North America, and in many ways we are always searching for ways to fuse the values of East and West. In particular, we have been attracted to the Asian tradition of non-linear thought and holistic thinking rather than the more regimented logic of the Western intellectual tradition.

Almost everybody in Vancouver is here from somewhere else. Except for the First Nations inhabitants, we are all recent immigrants. That's something that we've consciously tried to work into our office. That adds to the creativity. We like to say we get the best from Europe, the best from Asia, and the best from North America—it all comes together here with a staff of forty-five people, speaking twenty languages. Everybody brings a unique point of view. That synthesis of culture and ideas and viewpoints is one way we keep our ideas fresh. It can also mean language problems and cultural biases, but luckily we share the common language of drawing.

In a city this young you're not afraid to make mistakes. That appeals to the many creative individualists who run away to Vancouver. Why else are these runaways here? Well, because they hold a certain set of values that are beyond

*Michael Skapinker, "There Is More to City Life Than Convenience," *Financial Times*, June 29, 2009.

materialism. To demonstrate: Vancouver was ranked by *The Economist* as the number one city in the world for livability in 2009*, but when the consultancy A. T. Kearney combined rankings for livability *and* doing business, the city did not even make the top sixty. We don't do business here in the conventional way. In most big cities, you are under so much pressure to come up with quick solutions. Here we're not in the center of the storm. In Vancouver, you have time to think about things a little bit deeper. Our culture is prepared to value things like spiritualism and the environment—things that traditional business operations simply don't think about.

We're also not burdened by history: Vancouver is a city that has really been built in just the last fifty years. Compared to European cities and even older North American cities, here we often find a blank canvas. You can look at things from first principles. Not all your cues have to come from what already exists around you. Asking the question, "Why not?" is easier for us. When you give people a chance to do something unique without concerns about what has been done in the past, you get interesting results.

Climate affects how people think, and Vancouver's climate probably affects us more than we realize. But it's not about the rain; half the year, Vancouver can be gray, overcast, and moody, but also poetic and philosophical. It creates a certain atmosphere that encourages contemplation. That affects the way we think about architectural problems. For our work in Texas, where the sun is so strong, we've found people there seem to think more in terms of black and white than in Vancouver, where we see more shades of gray. The colors we use here in the Pacific Northwest have to be more subtle. Maybe that's one reason we like concrete as a building material so much. Whenever we begin any project, the first thing we do is try to see the local colors.

Our sense of proportion is also very different because of where we come from. Take Texas for example again, looking at the horizon, where two thirds of your view is sky, it's very different than Vancouver where two thirds is mountain. It's a different way of looking at the earth, of looking at your place in society. In Texas, where the sky is dark blue and the earth is almost bleached white, forms are much

clearer against the sky. In Vancouver, where the earth is dark and the overcast sky is white with reflected light, you have to finish a building against the sky with stronger gestures, otherwise you can't clearly see where the building ends and the sky begins.

Here, the mountains and the sea are huge influences on us too. We live on narrow strips of land, like tightrope walkers, wedged between the Coast Mountains and the Pacific Ocean. Because we're crunched together, the idea of mixed-use architecture—combining unlikely uses, stacked on top of each other—seems logical. And not only do we have water coming down on us for much of the year, we are surrounded by the sea, making it part of our psyche. Our city planners have connected Vancouver with its water's edge so successfully that there is now a word for it in European planning schools: Vancouverism. Our office is one block from the ocean, and in most of our own projects we look for opportunities to connect to water, whether it's the seaport of Dalian in China or a river channel in Fort Worth.

In every project outside Vancouver we're always asking questions: "How is it different here? What is the color of the earth here? How is the light coming into the building?" Sunlight is such a valuable commodity in the Pacific Northwest that it's something we're very sensitive to, particularly how light comes into a space and how we can use it.

Greenpeace was founded in Vancouver and it is also home to Dr. David Suzuki, both giants in the international environmental movement. That doesn't necessarily mean that the city is a global leader in sustainability, but that heritage does influence what we do as architects, from our use of natural materials to our own beliefs about sustainability. If you get overly enamored with green technology, it is easy to get distracted. We look beyond sustainability checklists to bigger questions, such as "How do we live together with the Earth, not just on it?" We don't assume every building should be demolished, or even built. To solve the environmental issues facing us, we are convinced that we have to re-evaluate the basic principles of human settlement. Cities are where the environmental problems we are facing will be solved.

We're not saying it's better here in Vancouver. We're just saying it is different.

Collisions

Making the most of every opportunity

Our passion is to improve the world, so we're often building in parts of cities that many people don't want to deal with. In a sense, we set out to build buildings that change society. We know that good architecture can change the trajectory of a community for the better, and that it will give people a sense of pride that is hard to replicate in any other way. The most exciting creative collisions happen in what we call "edge situations."

Curiously, it was an Austrian biologist who first sparked our interest in this possibility. Ludwig von Bertalanffy's *General Systems Theory* (1968) has its basis in the I Ching (we're always searching for ways to fuse Eastern and Western values), which is also tied to contemporary relativist thinking. His belief? That knowledge is to be found between the cracks rather than in the discipline itself. The most exciting research, for example, is often found not in biology or chemistry, but interdisciplinary sciences. University courses, for example, are being built around not just French or Japanese literature, but also comparative literature programs. Outside the classroom, any biologist knows that the richest areas on earth for ecological diversity are found in those margins between biozones. Riparian zones, the bogs and wetlands that are transition areas between aquatic areas and upland areas, are often referred to as "the ribbon of life."

How do an Austrian biologist's theories relate to architecture? Well, if you really want to change communities, you want to create collisions of mixed use. You look for edge cities, like Surrey, Vancouver's fastest growing suburb, with its endless highways, parking lots, shopping malls, and subdivisions. We wanted to create a new city center in one of Surrey's worst neighborhoods, an area with high poverty levels and student dropout rates. This project has been successful in large part because we were able to combine three unlikely destinations in one building: a

shopping mall, a major office tower, and a university campus. The identity created by this building has given the city new confidence that previously was missing. The result? Surrey has been energized to do more. The city council subsequently hired us to do a master plan that includes relocating their city hall—a fourth destination—to this new city center.

Fort Worth, Texas, is another example of changing communities for the better by looking beyond immediate problems. Water levels on the Trinity River have been rising and Fort Worth needed to update their flood control system. The obvious solution was to build new levees, but this is an enormous public expense. We were interested to see what we could do to leverage this considerable investment so that it would benefit the community beyond flood control. Rather than simply build new and higher levees, we proposed a bypass channel where floodwaters could be diverted during a catastrophic flood. Building on the theme of the river, we developed a plan organized around an urban lake and a series of canals. By controlling and channeling where the floodwaters go, our proposal effectively allowed six hundred acres of land adjacent to the downtown to be developed. Previously the threat of flooding had meant that there was very little building allowed. Now Fort Worth can welcome young families back into the center of the city, reversing the expansion of suburban sprawl. That urban design work led to a commission for us to help Tarrant County College (TCC) develop a new downtown campus.

As architects, probably the most sustainable thing we can do is increase density and encourage mixed use. Both fall under that very human value of trying to build a sense of community. For us, that's the number one priority: to give people a deeper sense of living together, in celebration. What makes a good community? If you're asking people to be content with less private space, then you have to give them more shared space—but it has to be great space, public space that they want to

use. In the suburbs, it's the opposite. Everyone has lots of private space, but there's no public space. So now we're asking, "How do we use public space to create a civil society, where people cherish communal values more than private values?"

Working in edge areas, we are always looking to break down barriers, sometimes these are physical, sometimes cultural. But for our firm, breaking down barriers always starts by looking at the whole city and seeing how a specific project fits. Arena Stage is a good example. In rebuilding its theaters, we also saw the chance to kick-start the redevelopment of Southwest Washington, D.C.

Everyone talks about change, how inevitable it is. We now realize a key part of renewing communities is looking at what has *not* changed. Whether it's in multicultural countries like Canada or melting pots like the United States, deep down, cultural change is much slower than we think. Look at Sunset in Vancouver. It's an immigrant neighborhood that has long been in transition. First we re-stitched the streets back to their old pattern, then we were able to move Sunset's new community center right next to the Punjabi Market action on Main Street.

In Richmond, a lively, mostly Asian suburb near Vancouver International Airport, we recognized that it was on the tipping point of becoming urban. We sped up the process with Aberdeen Centre, where we turned the traditional suburban shopping mall inside out. Aberdeen's multicolored glass exterior sits right on the sidewalk; cars are parked inside, out of sight.

Part of the appeal of designing for these edge conditions is our belief that a building is more than a utilitarian object: it needs to be beautiful, and that beauty only comes with the patina of age. In the past, architects tended to think that when a building is finished, it was at its perfect state of completion, that there should be no changes. But we believe that when you're designing, you have to think about how the building could get messed up. It's like buying a new wallet. When you buy it, it's stiff and rough. It's only with repeated use that the wallet becomes soft and supple. We get our true enjoyment as architects by seeing how people use the building as time goes by.

Jazz

We like to improvise and take inspiration from one another.

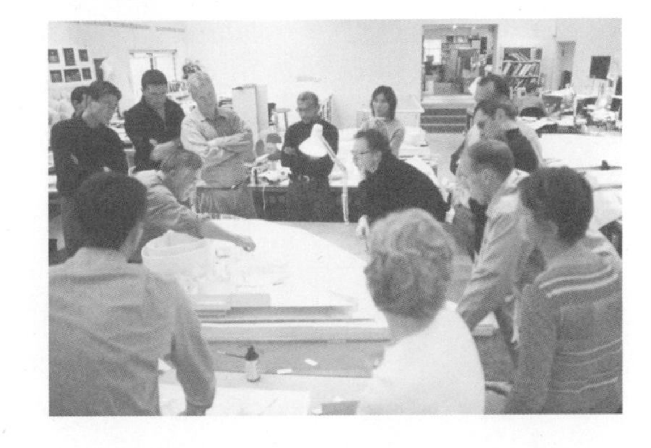

Ours is not an office where everything is decreed from above. Different people take the lead when they can, and relinquish it to the next person in a sort of back and forth. That's very much how we operate. Like a jazz band, it's always in this perpetual realm of improvisation, but it's in that call and response that creativity occurs. Most important, everyone has a chance to play. We like the fact there is no office style. Here, you're not given a manual and told you have to draw a certain way. There's no condescension where you're told what to do and how to execute the idea. The bottom line comes from the principals, but we probably give our staff more leeway than other firms.

When we're hiring, we look for people who are curious and who want to find new ways to do things. If they come with a passion for something else, as well as architecture, all the better. We've had architects and technicians equally skilled as puppeteers, physiotherapists, and anthropologists. We also look for people like our amazing technical colleagues, who ask, "Why not?" Most technologists tell designers, "Oh, no, you can't do this, you can't do that." Ours immediately start thinking, "*How* can we do this?"

We do put a lot of emphasis on hiring younger people, because they are open-minded, work faster, and energize our work. When we work crazy hours the younger ones bounce back quicker. They're enthusiastic and more experimental. Like scientists, you have some of your freshest ideas in your twenties and thirties, but it also takes years to perfect your craft. In many ways we regard a certain side of our practice as a kind of graduate school. Young people come here to build their résumé with varied experiences. Some people stay for a while, but at a certain point, they want to fly on their own. You have to say, "OK, good luck." We take pleasure from their subsequent success and their ability to apply the lessons they learned

while they were with us. We are also very fortunate to have many dedicated colleagues who have worked with us for years; with them, we've developed a kind of shorthand that allows us to work together with incredible efficiency.

Our design team is far more than just our staff at BTA. One of the luxuries of larger commissions and working in international locations is that we get to work with some of the best engineers and specialty consultants in the world. By working with them, we have been able to raise the bar on our own work. We like to collaborate with artists too, who often don't have the ability to translate their ideas into reality, certainly not on a large scale. This was recently the case for the SAIT Polytechnic parking garage, where we partnered an artist with a cladding manufacturer and installer to create a customized screen with pixilated images of clouds. Similarly, for the Canada Pavilion at Spain's Expo '92, we collaborated with a holographic artist to recreate Canada's northern lights.

The Right Client

Finding the right fit with a client is critical. Without that fit, there is no project. If you want something different and you're willing to try it, then we're the architect for you. Conversely, if you already know what you want to do, then we're probably not right for you. We want clients who are willing to come on a journey with us. We often tell them that they will have the most fun they have ever had, but they will also work harder than they have ever worked before. We need clients who are as passionate about the work as we are.

The Heart of the Project: The Building

A building should deserve to be built. With that said, we are always trying to find a project's deep inner value. For example, what is the spirit that underlies the building? That spirit will have to drive the project, sometimes, as is the case with the Arena Stage, for as long as ten years.

We have always been intrigued by cities and a significant portion of the work we do relates to urban planning and design. Our architecture is always shaped by its context, and by context we don't just mean its physical setting, but also the surrounding social and economic circumstances it could potentially influence. Constructing a building is an expensive proposition, so we want our clients to be able to benefit from whatever surrounds the project. For instance, on our Central City project in Surrey, there were already lots of food outlets in the attached shopping mall, so the university didn't need to build a cafeteria. This attitude swings both ways: we also want our buildings to contribute to the community. Tarrant County College is a great example. Their new downtown site encourages pedestrians to travel through the campus—a new public route from downtown Fort Worth to the banks of the Trinity River.

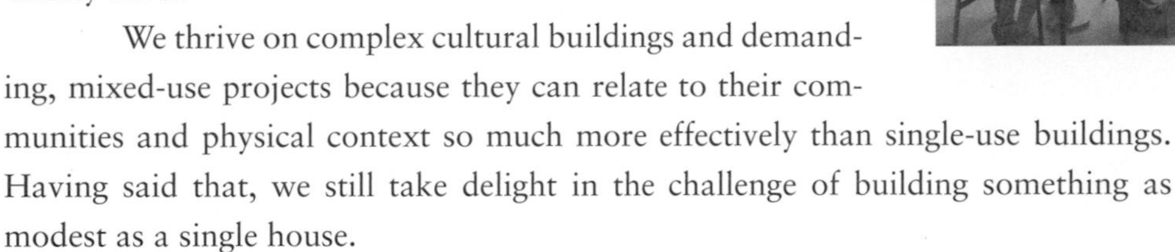

We thrive on complex cultural buildings and demanding, mixed-use projects because they can relate to their communities and physical context so much more effectively than single-use buildings. Having said that, we still take delight in the challenge of building something as modest as a single house.

Our Process

We like to start by asking the right question. Instead of asking, "What is a concert hall?" or "What is a university?" we ask, "What is listening to music?" and "What is learning?", the idea being that you start very big and set a general direction, opening a universe of possibilities. It's always evolving. Unfortunately, the building development process is very linear, so in the average architect's office, the emphasis is on getting the thing out. That's why there are so many mediocre buildings out there. As much as project managers like to claim otherwise, design is not a linear progression. The finesse is in managing the development process in such a way that there is room to ponder and explore. We like to spend a lot of time thinking, but ultimately there is pressure to produce a work of art. That's the hardest thing for young architects to understand. Every day you have to ask yourself, what have you done to advance this work of art?

But as any artist knows, there is no end to design. You can always make it better. Somewhere along the way, you just run out of time and you have to say that's it, but that doesn't mean it's perfection. We have to accept that. At that point we say, OK, stop talking and just draw. But even once a decision is made, it's always open to discussion later if there is an opportunity to significantly improve the design.

Our Base

We thought a lot when designing our own office building. Many architects (and architectural schools) over-design their offices. That inhibits their own creative process. We believe what works best is an older building that is not too precious. It should even be a bit scruffy, available for experimentation. Consequently, our office is an agglomeration of old buildings we linked together and built onto to create three studio/workshops. Although these spaces are rarely tidy, they give us the room and environment we need to work. It is definitely a workplace, not a showroom, to the initial surprise of some clients!

Our Tools

Drawing ability is the ultimate tool of the architect, but when you draw a line you're defining objects, while architecture is really about creating space. It's the space between the lines that creates the experience of being inside a building. We sometimes use the analogy of clothing. There's more to clothing than what a garment looks like. It's what happens when your arms or body are inside the clothing. How does it make you feel? Is it comfortable? Some people allow the clothes to wear them, instead of the other way around. It's the same with architecture.

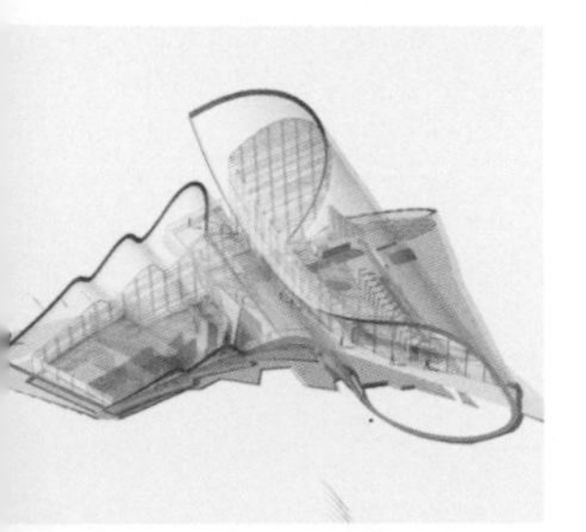

Like most design offices, we recognize the advantages of computer modeling, an art form of its own, and we make use of 3-D model printers and laser cutters that can produce a model in hours that would have taken days to hand build. Recently we used computer visualizations and 3-D model prints very effectively to design a proposal for a winery in the Okanagan Valley.

But despite the considerable advances in computer visualization, physical model making remains an integral part of our design process. We often begin with small-scale site models so that we can develop a thorough physical understanding of the site's context, starting with topographic models to get the lay of the land. Often these site models encompass whole sections of a city or landscape, and take up a big space in the studio. As the design progresses, the scale of the models increases so that we can study the various building components and, ultimately, details.

The act of physically building a model requires understanding of how things fit together. It gets you into the material world of glue, pins, and sticks, and breaks you away from drawing and computers, which can be therapeutic for everybody. You're standing up, walking around, turning your head, moving in space; you're free from that two-dimensional thinking that happens when your eye is always twelve inches from the screen. You learn about materials. The model also helps to give a sense of scale that you just don't get in a drawing. Sometimes we build models at different scales simultaneously to find the appropriate balance.

Models are a brilliant tool for communicating, and we always have a working model in the middle of the studio, with material samples, as a touchstone for the whole team. There is one danger: Because a model takes so long to build, it can become a treasured icon, but then it's no longer a useful design tool, so we often go out of our way to break the model down and change it, even if it's not necessary, just to break the habit of becoming fixated on a solution too quickly.

All firms build models, but it's rare to find one that builds them at full scale. We do, most of the time right in our parking lot, where we can see how they perform under different weather conditions. Whether we're trying to figure out how to build something, what it's going to look like, or how it's going to behave, we do this routinely, because we work with so many design-build components. It also helps that we have a coterie of craftsmen we work with who are willing to do it. We consider these mock-ups to be a way of reducing the risk, financially and aesthetically, of any innovative features in the design. It also gives the client a chance to really see what we're talking about instead asking them to imagine the real thing from a model or computer renderings.

In a sense, the houses we design are mock-ups too. We only do one house every few years, because they take so much time, so while we're at it, we like to treat them as R&D for larger projects; from the very beginning we tell the client, "We're going to experiment on your house." Houses are tools we can use to try things out without taking on the risk of a large scale installation, not to mention that they're a great way to train staff as well.

We've recently formalized the firm's keen focus on research and development by setting up BTAworks as a subsidiary R&D arm. The company analyzes data to help us better understand the demography and various trends in the communities we're working with. It also looks at architecture and sustainability holistically (we're more interested in how the forest works than the individual leaves on the trees). We want to get beyond LEED—it can be so hard to tell the "greenwashing" from the truth. Although the principles behind LEED are admirable, striving for certification can stifle innovation, which we feel the world needs now more than ever. Technical innovation is certainly critical, but it is also equally important to better understand our communities.

Chan Centre for the Performing Arts

In the Chan Centre for the Performing Arts, we faced challenges in both the interior and the exterior. It's important to keep in mind that when you design a concert hall, you are actually designing a reverberation chamber, a sort of extension of the musical instrument itself. You are designing, essentially, the inside of a violin. However very often, as architects, we become overly preoccupied with the violin case. We forget that ultimately it is the violin that is important. We sought to apply this principle to the Chan Centre.

Inside, we collaborated with the world's best acousticians and theater consultants to achieve the finest sound possible for concerts, music, and drama. But acoustics are not all about audio measurement. On another level, they are as much about what you *think* you hear as what you actually hear. The feeling of the room must add to that total acoustical experience. If the visual is not there to reinforce the acoustical experience, it actually distracts from it. That's why, very often, people listening to music close their eyes. You hear better. So, as architects, how do you inspire people with the feeling and surrounding of what we call "visual acoustics"? Visual acoustics are about a room not only being full, but feeling full; being intimate, but being grand, as well.

One of the characteristics of concert halls is that they are really big. Our first challenge was to set this big box (our violin case) within the site and make it disappear as much as possible. It is a very sensitive site adjacent to the ceremonial Flag Plaza entrance at the University of British Columbia. We also had to consider that the Chan would be eight stories high, whereas most campus buildings are only three or four. Most concert halls are big boxes against urban backdrops, but the Chan is in a sylvan setting at the heart of the university. The site is in the middle of a small forest of beautiful cedars and firs, mixed in with some two hundred azaleas and rhododendrons.

One of the first things the university instructed us to do was to cut down all the trees, so patrons could see the ocean and the mountains. We pointed out that at night, when the facility would primarily be in use, you wouldn't see the view. With many of the trees over one hundred years old we were counting on their height to mitigate the enormous scale of the building. We chose to play up the trees rather than cut them down. In the evening, when the sun goes down, we light them up so that when the audience comes out during the intermission they find themselves amidst a magical forest. In addition to saving the trees, we tagged all the rhododendrons when they were in bloom so we knew what color they were, then stored them in the university nursery to replant after the building was constructed. Ultimately only one tree had to fall—it was in the middle of the road.

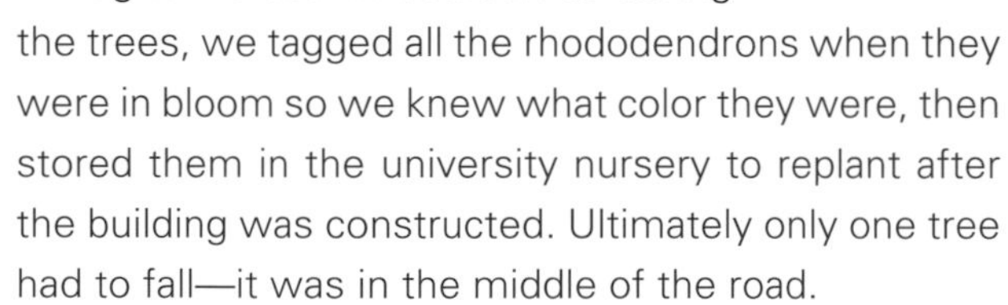

It's wonderful when musicians tell us the Chan is one of the world's best concert halls, but we know the Chan is really a success when someone in the audience says, "It feels like a musical instrument!" These are the best compliments you can have as an architect—from people who independently discover the essence of the building.

E PERFORMING ART

Site plan

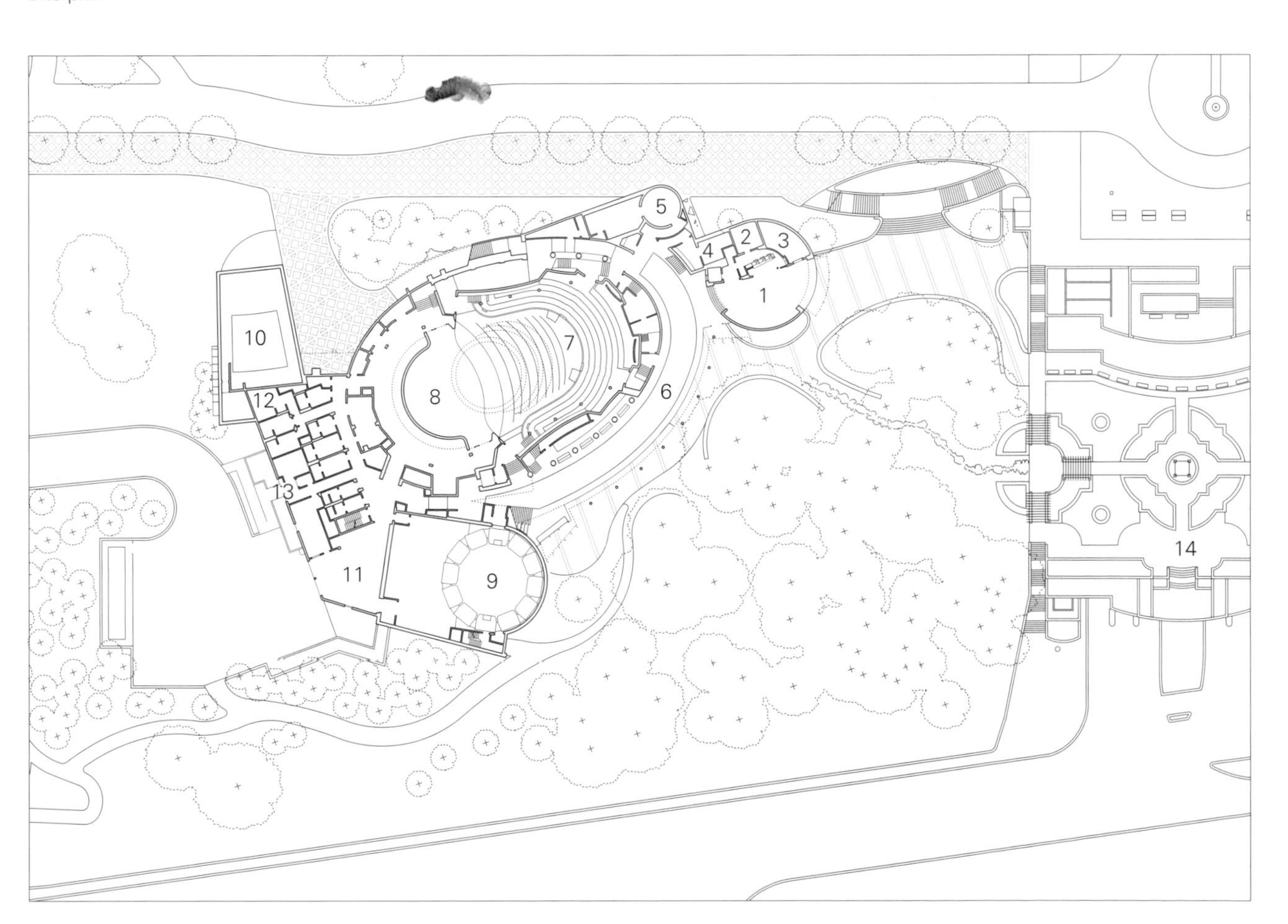

Floor 1 plan

1. Foyer
2. Ticket office
3. Coats
4. Men's restroom
5. Women's restroom
6. Lobby
7. Concert hall
8. Stage
9. Studio theater
10. Cinema above
11. Loading and receiving
12. Dressing rooms
13. Stage door
14. Rose garden

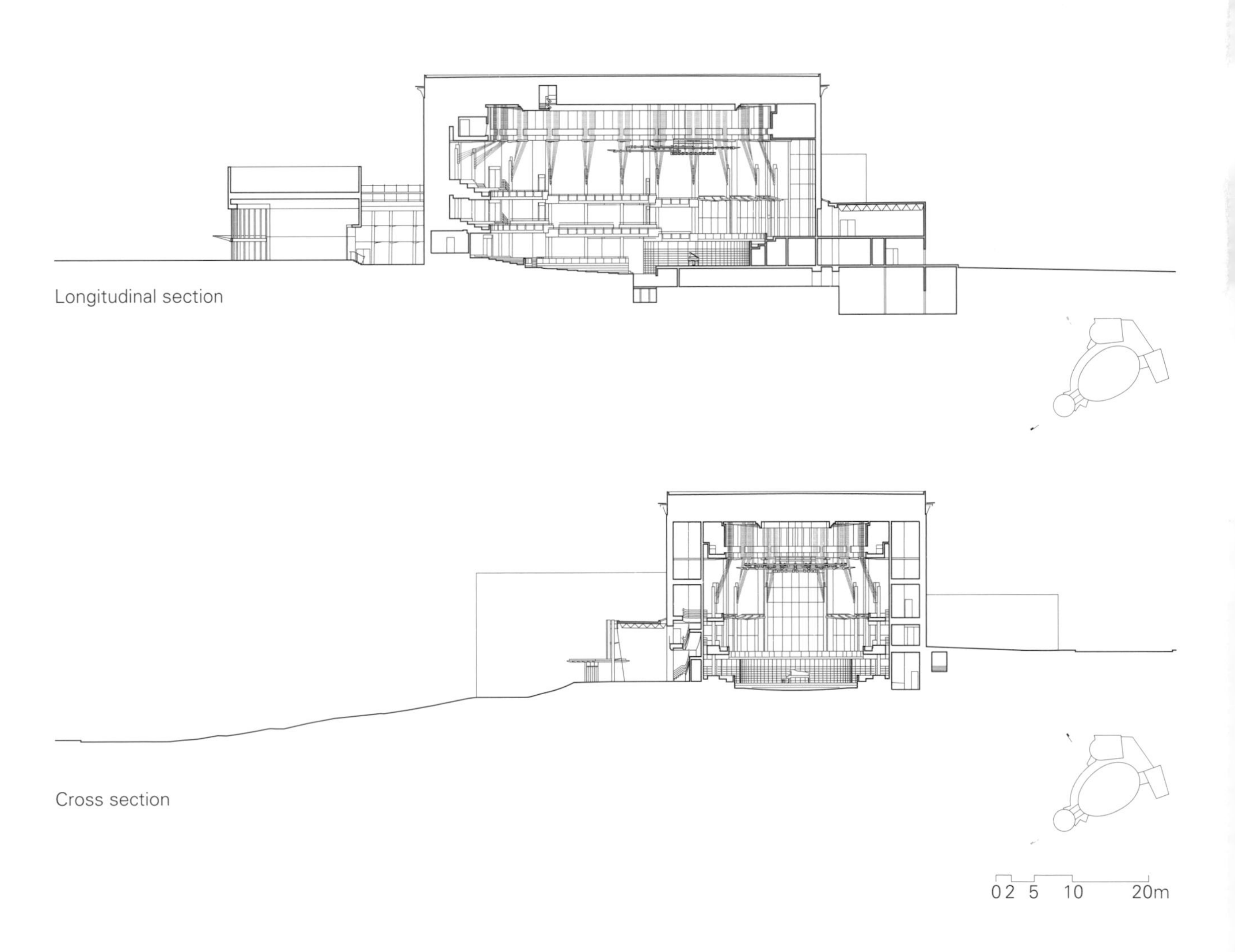

Longitudinal section

Cross section

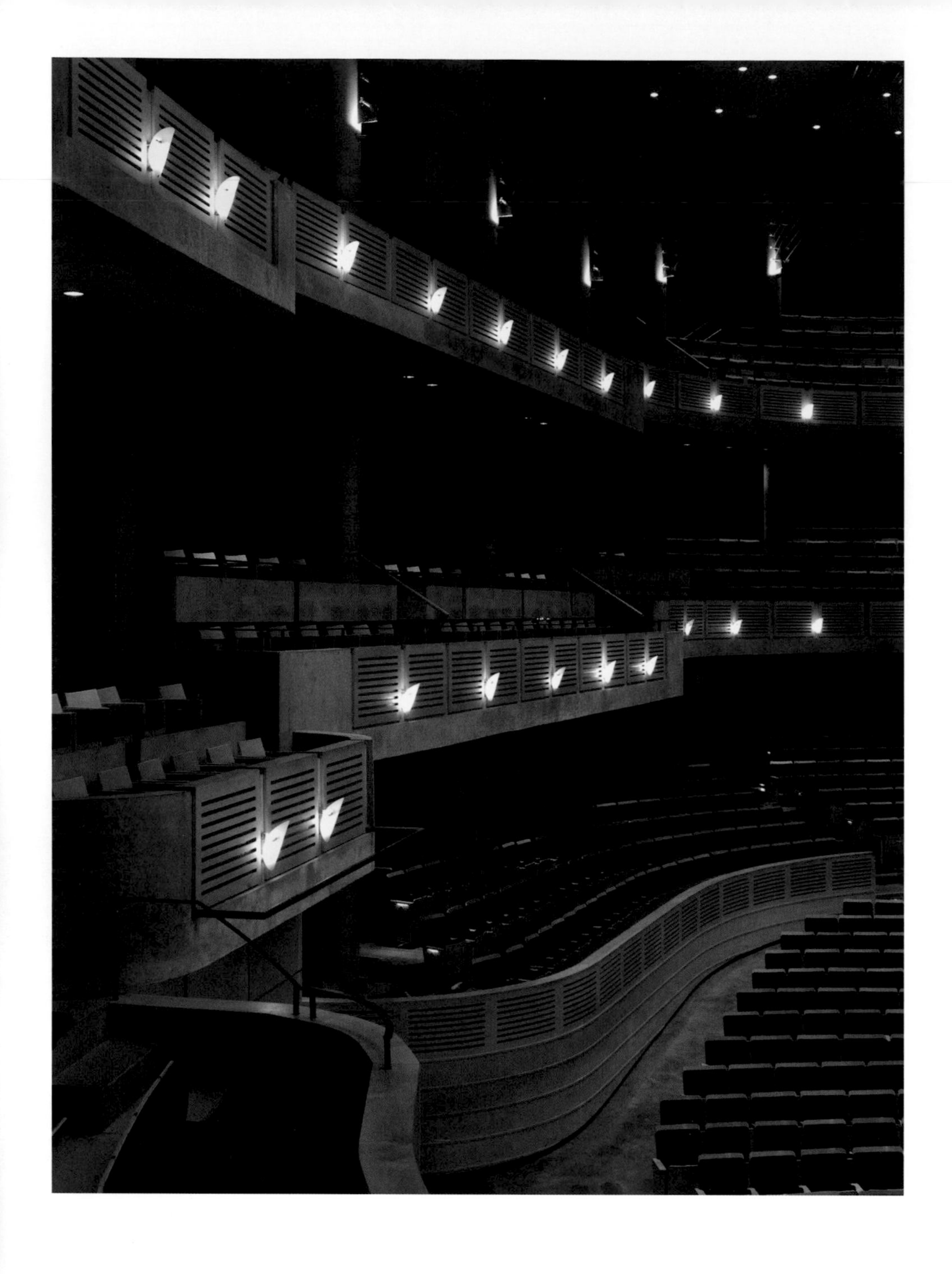

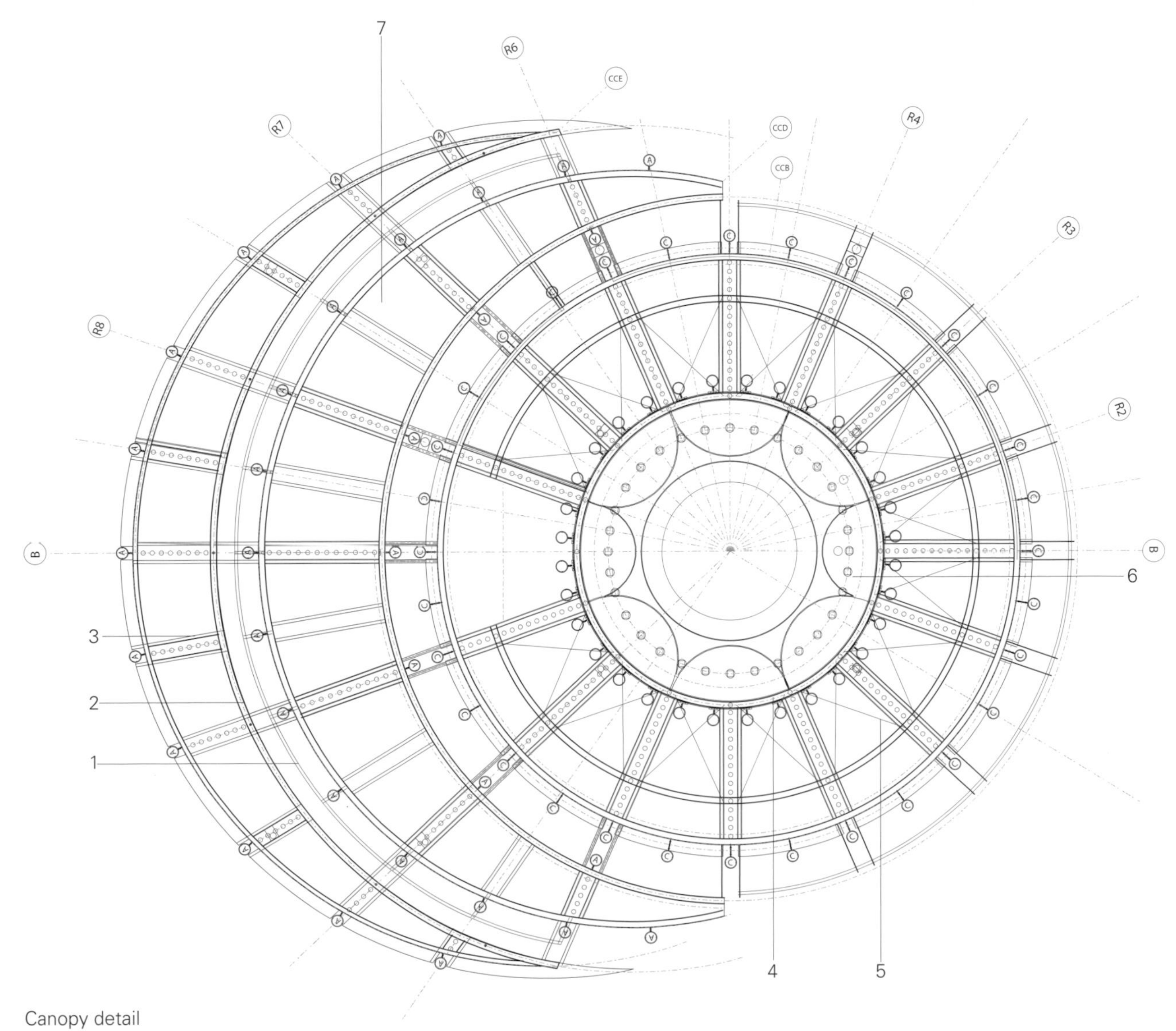

Canopy detail

1. Light pipe
2. HSS steel frame
3. Radial glass rib and lighting strip
4. Steel pipe frame
5. SS cables
6. Gold leaf on plywood
7. Silver leaf on plywood

HAN CENTRE FOR THE

Surrey Central City

Surrey is a suburban edge city on the southern boundary of metro Vancouver. It's a young, sprawling city of highways, parking lots, and shopping malls that is the frequent butt of jokes. It struggles with lower education and income levels than elsewhere in the region. Yet because land is plentiful and inexpensive, Surrey is growing faster than almost any other city in Canada. Because Vancouver can only expand south into Surrey, and is constrained geographically, in the not-too-distant future the population of Surrey will likely top Vancouver's.

Set on a peninsula surrounded on three sides by mountains and ocean, Vancouver is stunningly beautiful, but hugely limited. Its eccentric unidirectional growth is also incredibly inefficient from a transportation point of view. Recognizing this, over thirty years ago, metro Vancouver developed what become known as the Livable Region Plan. Central to this plan is the creation of a series of town centers that would take some of the pressure off of Vancouver's downtown and allow people to live and work in closer proximity. To encourage this development, in the 1980s planners linked many of the town centers by a rapid transit system called Skytrain. The largest of these proposed town centers was for Surrey, the first municipality south of the Fraser River. Once Skytrain was built, a series of high-profile planners were engaged to develop a vision for the new town center, but nothing really took shape. Surrey Centre was an architects' graveyard of ideas. There was no "downtown Surrey," it was Nowhere, North America.

How do you create the beginning of a city center when you're presented with all this suburban sprawl? How do you create architecture that gives people pride, dignity, and a sense of the future? We believed that a large mixed-use development with a significant public-sector component could kick start Surrey's missing downtown. We were very lucky that we had three enlightened clients: provincial, municipal, and private, all with very different needs, but willing to work together and compromise.

To put it all in context, we had a major insurance company that was looking for both a regional head office and real estate investment opportunities, while Simon Fraser University needed a new campus, and Surrey needed a town center. Initially we were able to broker a deal between the city and provincial government, whereby in exchange for the city donating land in the designated city center, the province would agree to locate the new university there. We were also doing work for a large insurance company that was looking for real estate investment opportunities for their financial reserves. We suggested that they might want to option the shopping center that was for sale across the street from where the new university was supposed to go.

This part of the city, known as Whalley, was arguably the bleakest part of Surrey, despite being on the rapid transit line. The project was already complex and could have been a tough sell. But by sheer luck, we had a remarkably informed client in the chairman of the insurance corporation, Bob Williams. A planner by training as well as a former politician, Bob immediately recognized the value of creating a city center, but he wasn't convinced the project made sense. Then one weekend he checked out the area

Site plan

and was profoundly affected by the social challenges in Whalley. When he came back he said, "This community has been shortchanged for generations. If we can get one student lining up at university enrollment instead of in the unemployment line, then we will have done something." In the end, the insurance company bought the shopping center and, at the request of the provincial government, agreed to act as the developer for both the university and a new office building. This was tremendously exciting because we now had the main ingredient we needed to get a city center going: people.

The shopping mall, while considered to be in decline, was still generating over 1,400 visits per hour, the university would introduce 5,000 students, and the office building another 2,500 workers. We decided to integrate the different uses as closely and as much as we could. We proposed literally ripping the roof off the shopping center, and then we placed the university classrooms above it. It sounds strange to put a university on top of a shopping center, but now when you're shopping, you look up, and there are hundreds of students changing classes every hour. By combining the energy of the shopping center and the university, we also saved both capital and operations costs. For example, the university didn't need to build a cafeteria because the students can just use the mall's food court. Similarly, instead of building their own athletic facilities, the university gives each student a membership to the city's recreation center across the street. There were huge opportunities to reduce the need for parking as well. Since the peak parking requirements for a shopping mall occur in the evenings, weekends, and during the busy Christmas season, i.e., times when the university is closed, they can share parking the rest of the time.

We created a series of atria to organize the building around. To celebrate and to give distinctive common identity to these spaces we decided to use heavy timber construction—a technique historically associated with British Columbia—in a contemporary, high-tech way that would reflect the technology focus of the university. We entered into a design-build arrangement with a local wood fabricator and developed three distinct timber systems, including a wood-space frame constructed from peeler-cores (a waste product from the plywood industry). We also created a civic plaza, the first truly urban, civic, and open space in Surrey. We aligned the plaza with the mall entrance that faced the Skytrain. It has become the de facto entrance to the university and the complex as a whole, with thousands of pedestrian commuters crossing it each day.

The project is tremendously popular. This new generation of students, many working part-time, like being integrated into the community; it's more like real life. Even though the Surrey campus has only been open a few short years, and has far fewer resources than the main Simon Fraser University campus, Surrey actually has a longer waiting list to get in.

This is a wonderful example of the power of good architecture. This building has changed the trajectory of Surrey. It has given the community a new sense of confidence, and there's no longer any argument about where the center is. The city is now planning to build civic facilities like a library and city hall next door and has changed its logo from a crest to a profile of our building. And Whalley, once mocked, has rebranded itself as Downtown Surrey.

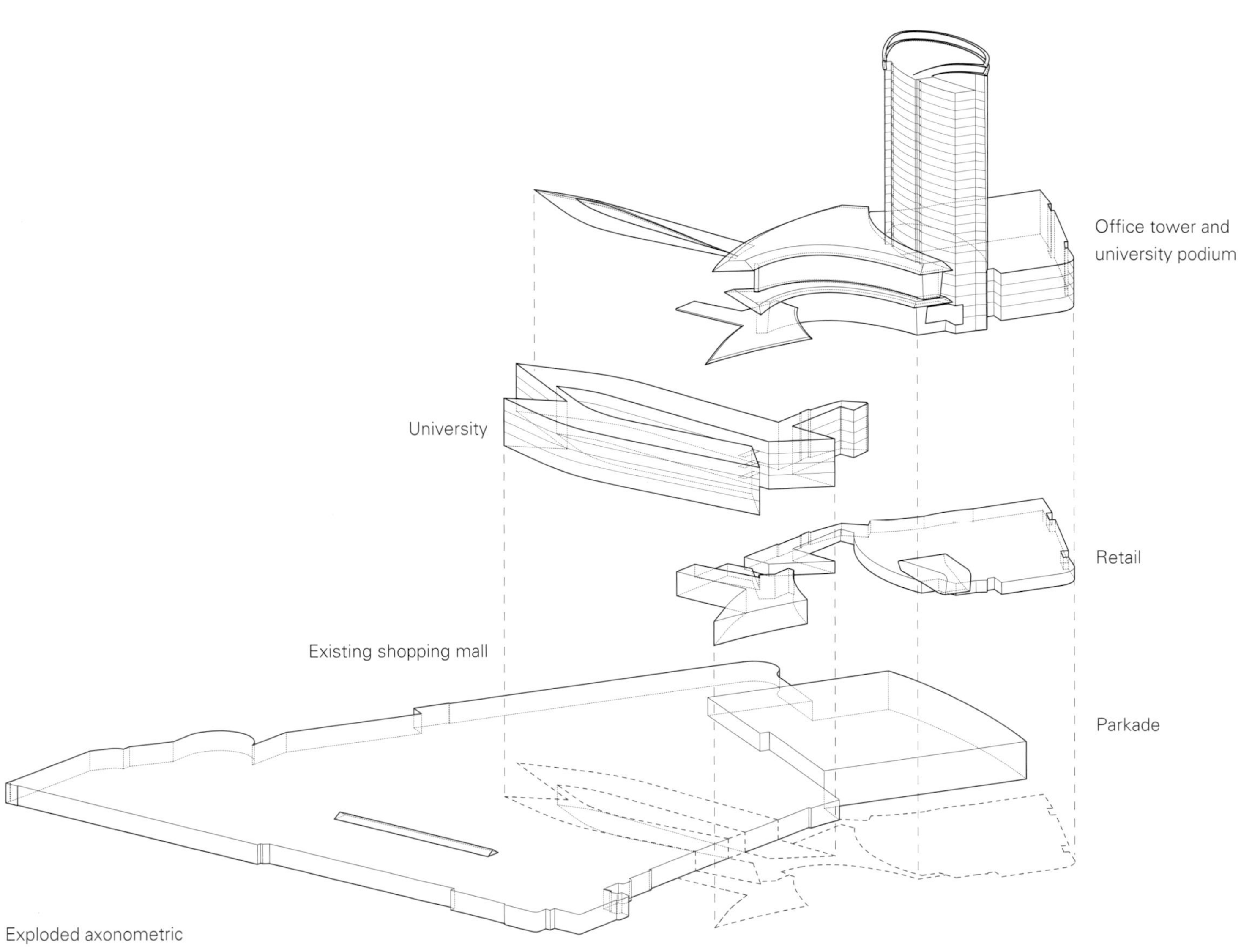

Exploded axonometric

13450
102 Avenue

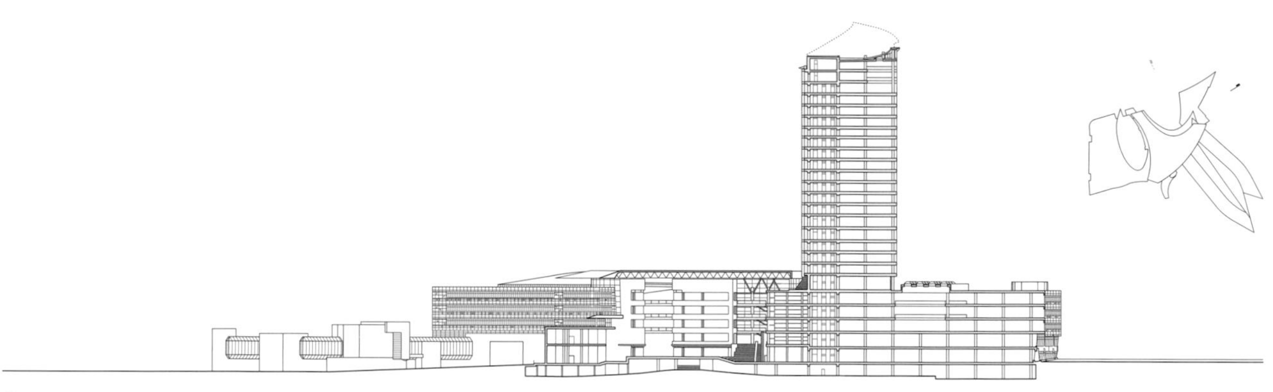

Cross section

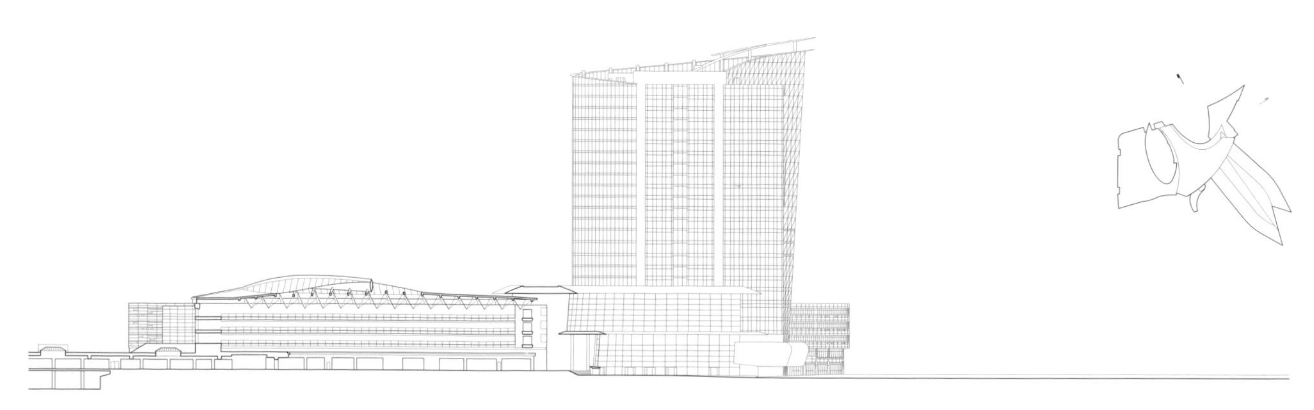

Longitudinal section

0 10 20 50 100m

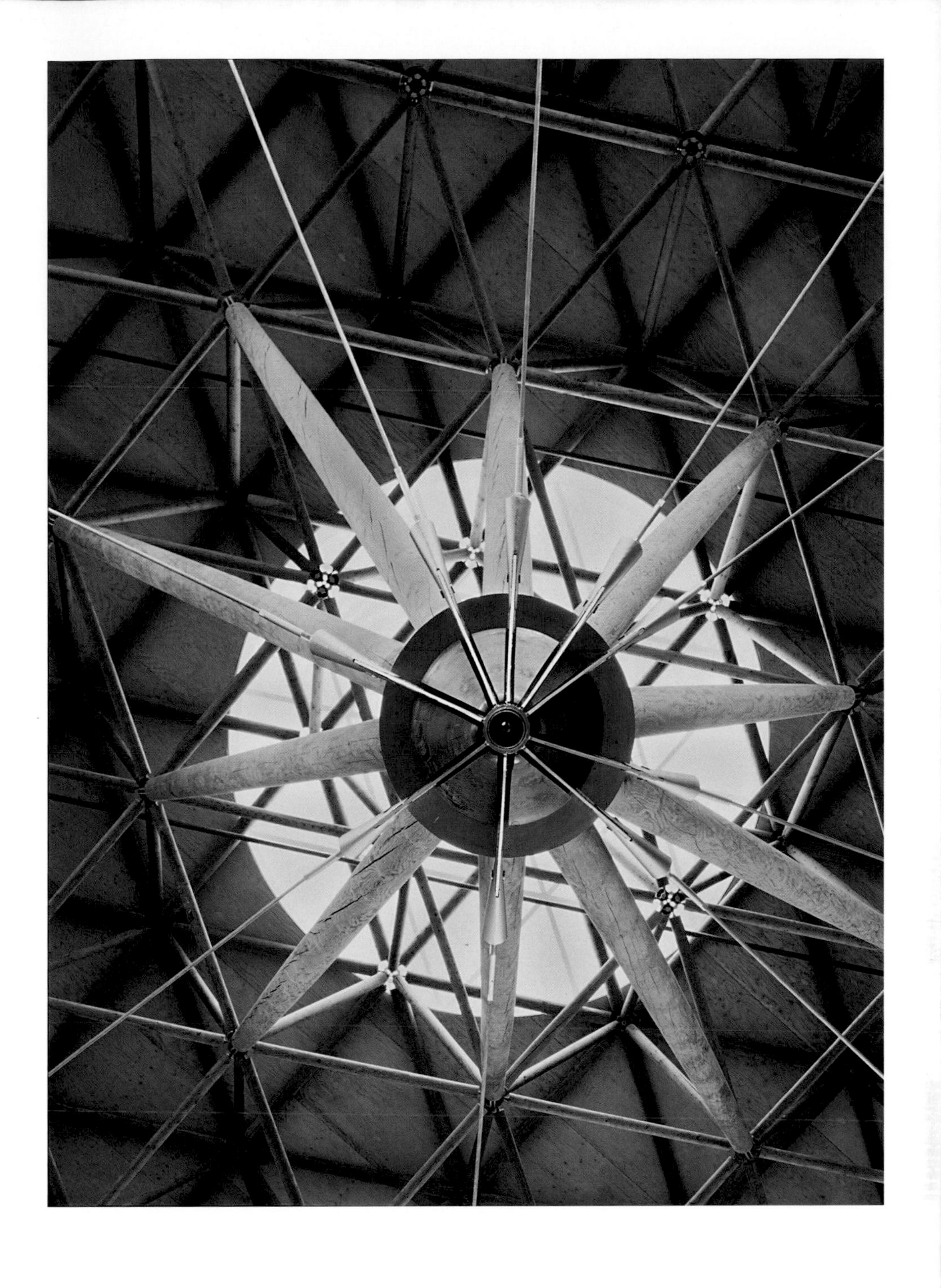

TY SURREY

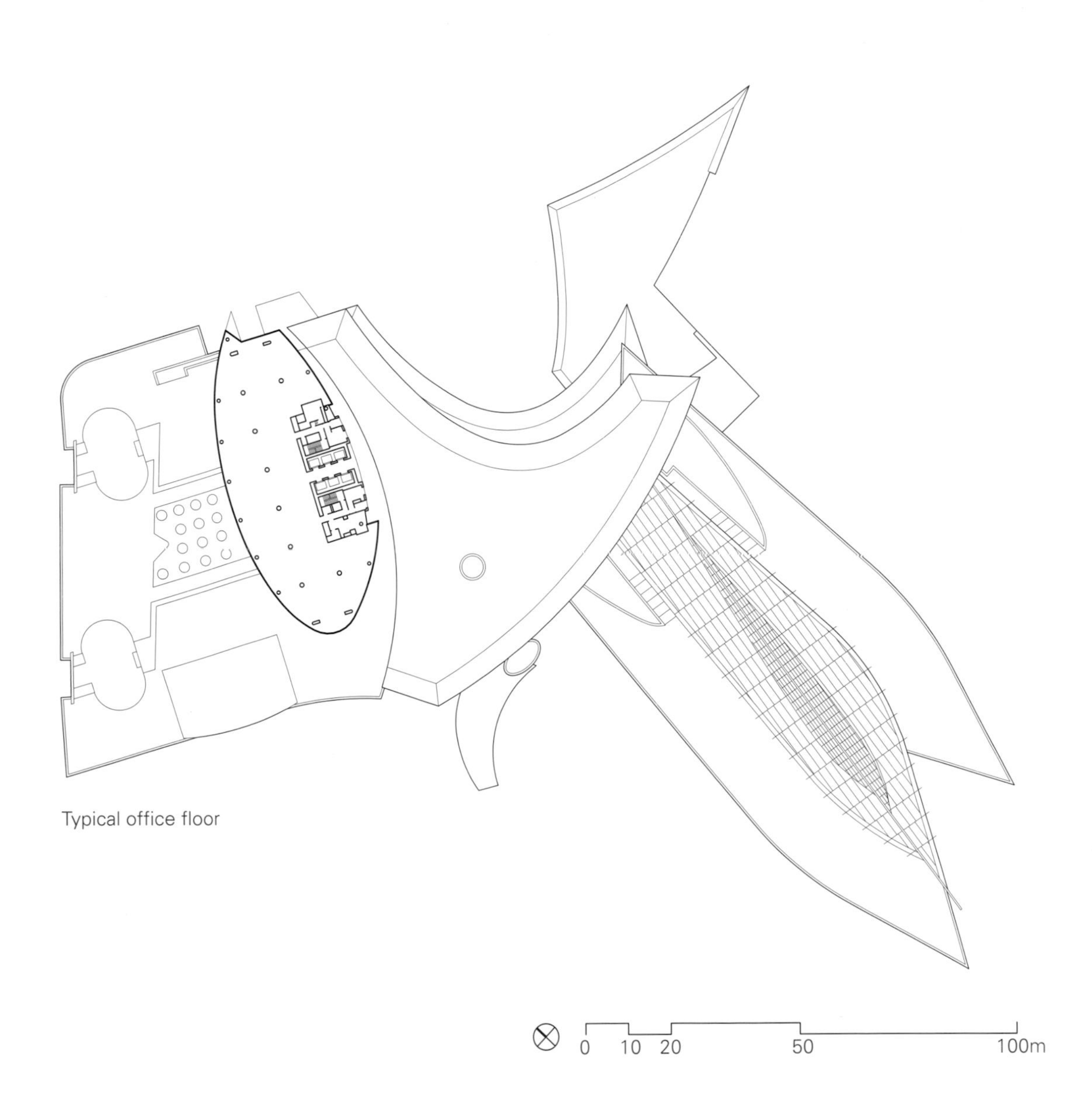

Typical office floor

Gismondi's

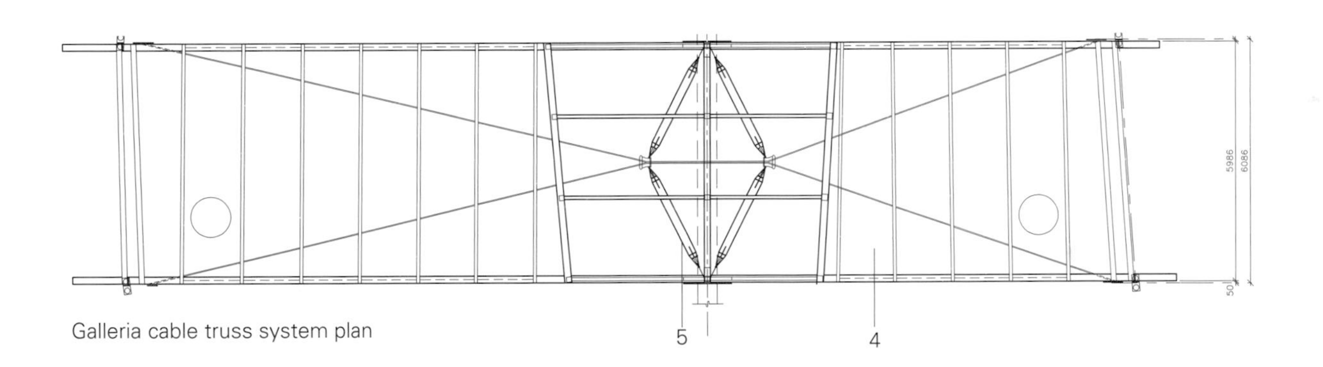

Galleria cable truss system plan

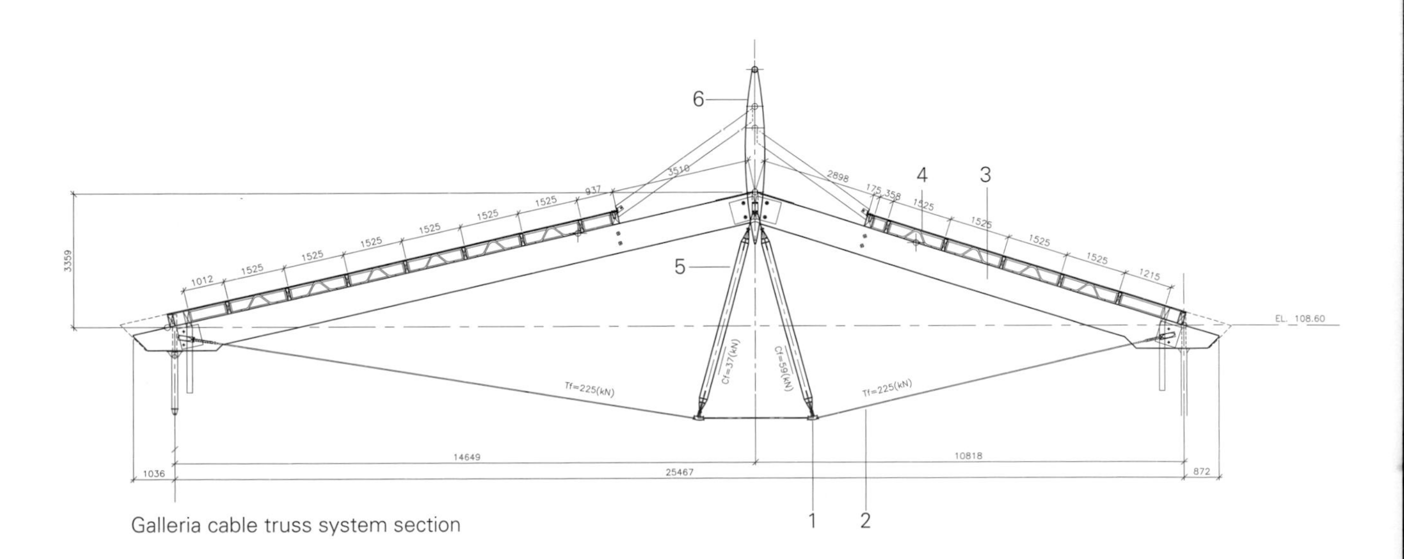

Galleria cable truss system section

1. Custom steel connectors
2. Steel cable
3. Glulam members
4. Plywood on timber purlins
5. Round peeler core struts
6. Plywood on timber frame continuous rib

Aberdeen Centre

Suburban shopping centers are not a building type that we have ever had much interest in. Many in the office hate those found in most cities because they're designed to get you lost. They're like mazes, and you can't find your way out. Ironically, our ambivalence toward shopping centers was actually considered an advantage by our client, who wanted us to reinvent the suburban mall. As a result, our design was an extension of the city streets, where you can always find your way out. At the same time, the interior environment has enough excitement with light and people moving through the space that you want to stay inside.

The city of Richmond is a typical suburb built on farmland. Since the 1960s, it has been all about traditional suburban shopping centers, with shops and anchor stores typically surrounded by a sea of surface parking. But we had confidence that this Vancouver suburb with its principally Asian population was maturing. We wanted to give people a new urban center. The client wanted a globalized shopping mall, free of North American chain stores. While we designed the building, he literally shopped the world for specialty stores.

In Aberdeen, we broke all the conventions of suburban shopping mall design. We turned it inside out, providing the same amount of parking in an aboveground structure cocooned *inside* the shopping center. That's how we were able to bring Aberdeen's new facade right up against the street. The form of the building then took its inspiration from the major curve of that street. Inside, we created a lively series of curving "streets" and courtyards that are anchored by restaurants and

food courts, rather than the traditional department stores found in most malls. To bring daylight in, we punctuated the ceiling with beautiful, deep cones, specifically angled so that they bring in natural light without allowing the sun to directly shine on and damage merchandise.

Where most shopping malls are blank boxes, we designed the building like a playful glass lantern, so Aberdeen Centre would light up at night—the kind of lantern that painter Piet Mondrian would have appreciated, we like to think. After all, his colorful, geometric *Broadway Boogie Woogie* (1943) was one of our inspirations. In the daytime, especially on rainy, gray winter days, the colors of Aberdeen's luminous wall cladding are equally as eye-catching as they are inviting.

Because the city of Richmond agreed that we could put the mandatory public art budget toward the innovative building cladding—something it had never done before—we were able to experiment with a local glazing company to create a new technique that imbeds translucent film into the glass. That's what gives Aberdeen's unique street front its joie de vivre. The whole shopping center has become public art.

Site plan

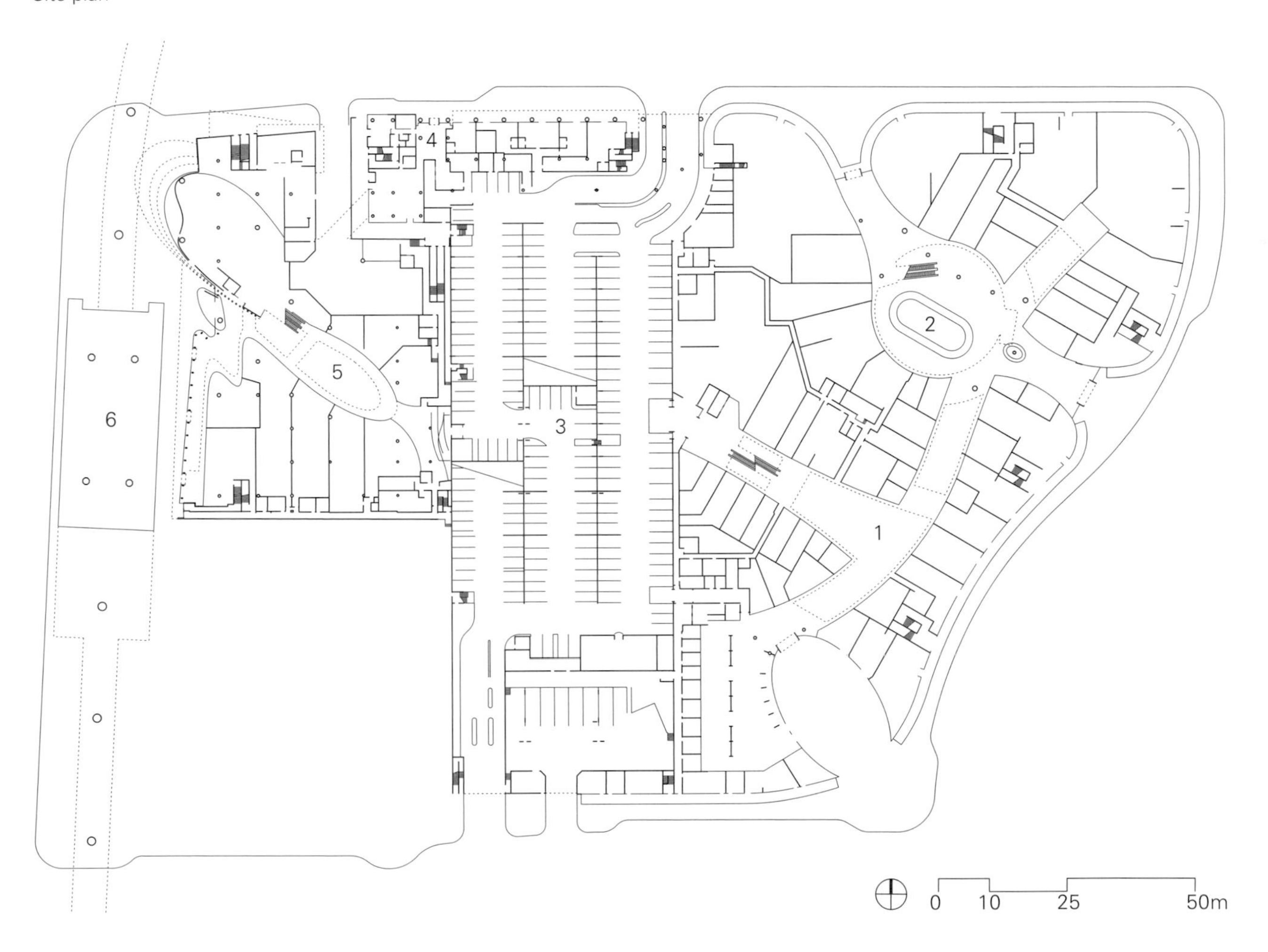

Ground-level plan

1. Shopping center (phase 1)
2. Fountain
3. Parking garage
4. Condominiums lobby (phase 2)
5. Aberdeen Station Lands shopping center (phase 3)
6. Rapid transit station

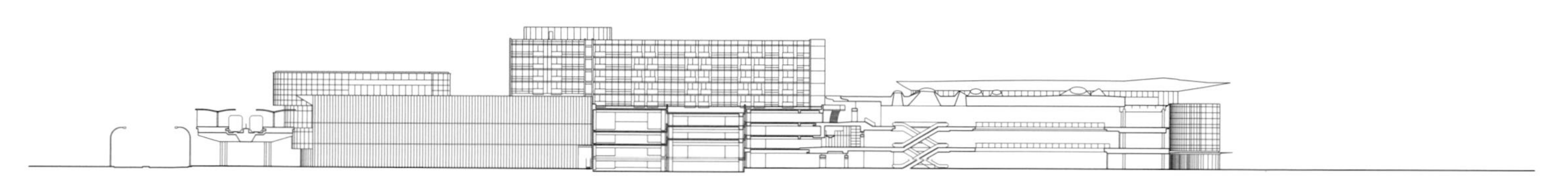

Cross section

0 10 20 50 100m

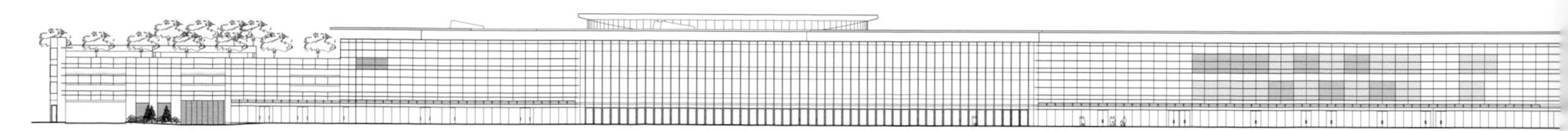

Unfolded elevation

HAZELBRIDGE WAY

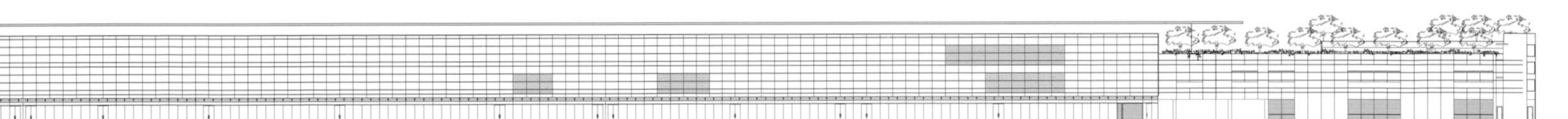

EXIT

Sunset Community Centre

Vancouverites love their distinct neighborhoods. The city consciously cultivates neighborhood identity, and community centers are a key ingredient to achieving that. Like many of Vancouver's communities, Sunset is a neighborhood in transition. Historically, it has always been an immigrant neighborhood. Germans arrived after World War II; now it's a mix of mostly South Asians, some Chinese, and the remaining Europeans. When we first talked to neighborhood residents, people complained that there wasn't anywhere big enough for their typically large Indian weddings. It didn't help that the old community center was set too far away from Main Street, the main drag of what's called Punjabi Market: a mix of Indian restaurants, jewelers, specialty food stores, clothing, and fabric shops that draws people from all over Vancouver.

The old community center was on a very large site, about the equivalent of six city blocks, owned by the Vancouver Park Board. The site included an elementary school and a large plant nursery in the middle that was completely fenced off, blocking the original streets. The first thing we proposed was to take down as much fence as possible and re-stitch most of the city blocks back into their original pattern. Then we could integrate the various activities on the site and we could build Sunset's new community center right next to all the action on Main Street. We wanted the building to be both a crossroads and a gateway. People can cut through the Centre on their way to the school, checking out activity in the plant nursery on their way. It's a natural short cut. Inside the Centre, people now walk

along two "streets" that cross each other, checking out their neighbors who are busy in the gym, yoga room, day care, craft areas, and multipurpose rooms for seniors. We kept all the earth we excavated on the site and used it to create rolling berms beside the building, so that the roof forms appear to come out of the landscape, with the building hugging the ground beneath.

In terms of the building form, we wanted a playful building that would stand out in its setting of generally subdued, modest homes. We also wanted to play off of the exuberance of the Punjabi Market up the street; our hope was that the building would come alive in a special way during all the colorful festivals and parades that originate there. We initially took our inspiration from the plants in the nursery and created five roofs, curved like leaves or petals. It's interesting that other people look at the roofs and see a sari floating in the air. Regardless, we were playing on that very fleeting moment when you catch sight of something wonderful and think, "Wow! Where did that come from?"

And the weddings? We designed a very grand room facing Main Street for receptions and other community events. Membership went up by forty percent within weeks of the new Centre opening. For really big celebrations, like Canada Day, people spill outside, using the bermed ground as natural amphitheaters. Even better, festival processions can parade right through the building and assemble in the adjacent park outside.

Site plan

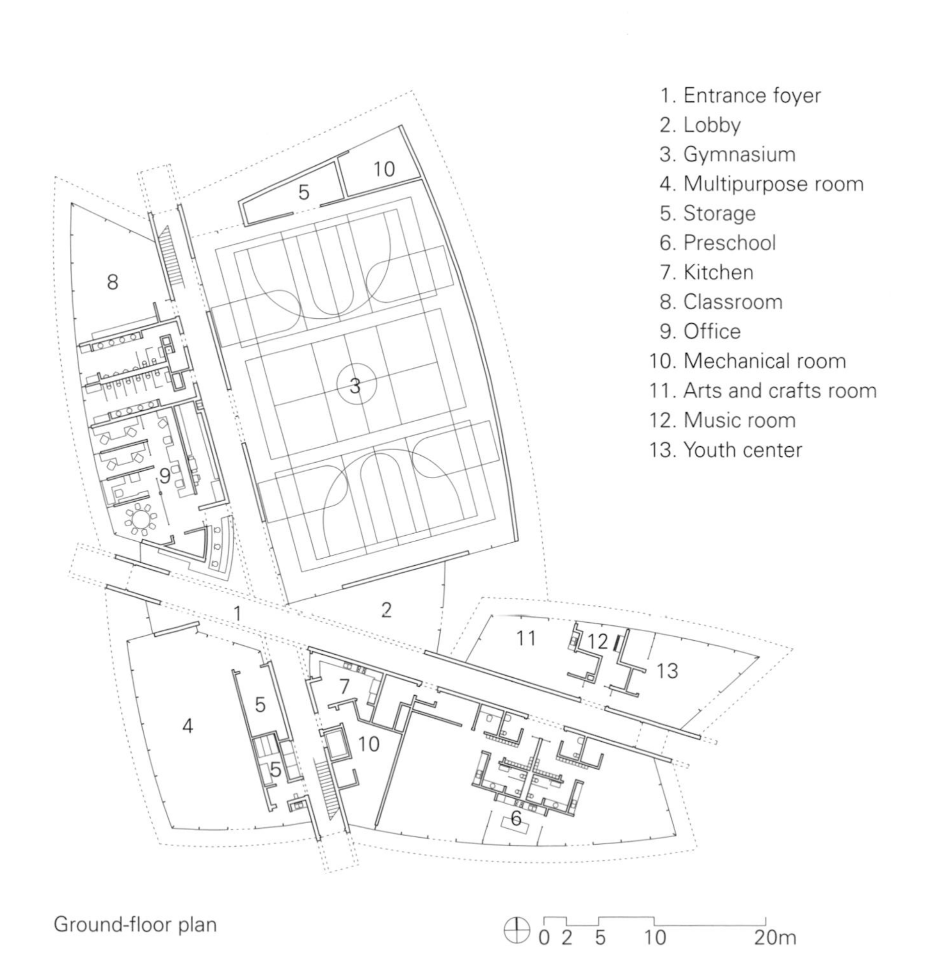

1. Entrance foyer
2. Lobby
3. Gymnasium
4. Multipurpose room
5. Storage
6. Preschool
7. Kitchen
8. Classroom
9. Office
10. Mechanical room
11. Arts and crafts room
12. Music room
13. Youth center

Ground-floor plan

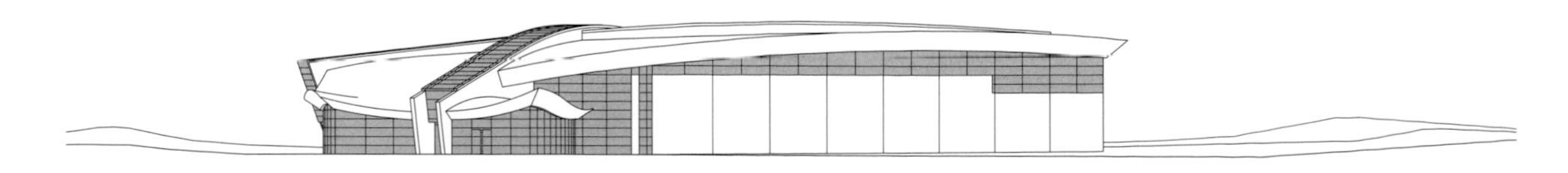

East elevation

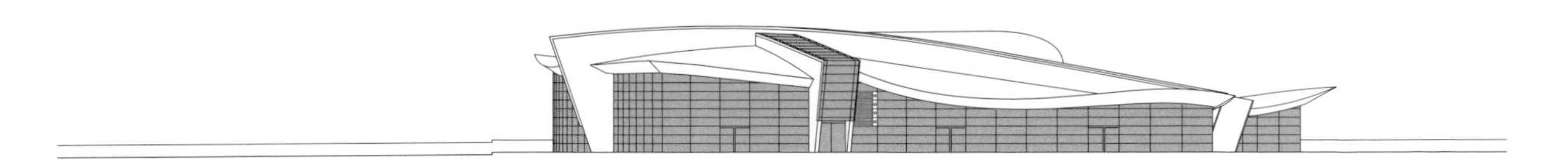

South elevation

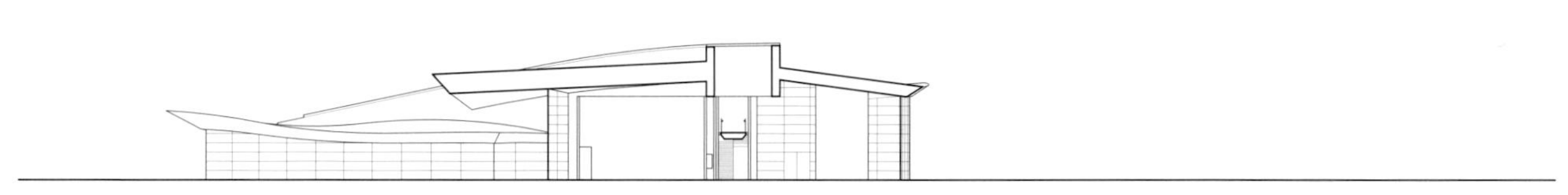

Cross section 1

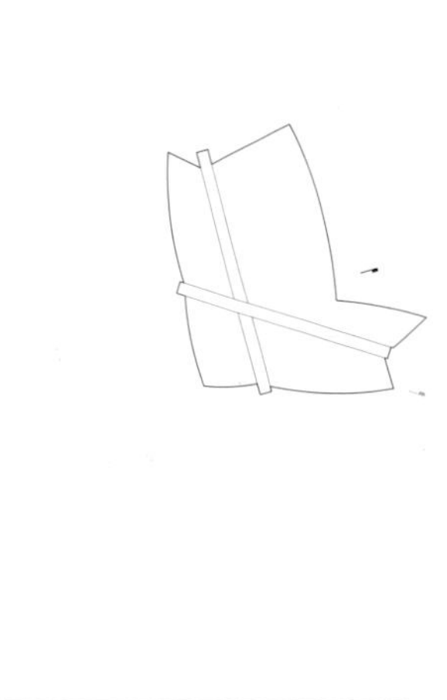

Cross section 2

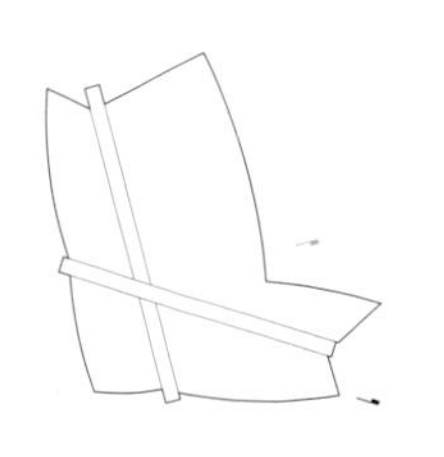

0 2 5 10 20m

EXIT

Tarrant County College

When we received the commission to design a new downtown campus for Tarrant County College (TCC) we were thrilled. Here was an opportunity to start implementing the Trinity Uptown Vision plan that we had been working on for downtown Fort Worth. That plan looked to transform six hundred flood-prone acres into an inner city waterfront neighborhood for some ten thousand young families. We knew this residential community would encourage young families to move back into the city, but we also felt strongly that it needed a significant educational institution that would anchor the new downtown community.

The Tarrant County College District (TCCD) are a visionary bunch, and in reviewing the needs of their community, the board saw a large population near downtown Fort Worth that was characterized by low income and low levels of education. This largely Hispanic community is still not totally integrated into the larger population. Physically, they've been separated from Fort Worth's downtown business community by the Trinity River, and access to higher education was an even bigger barrier to the future for Hispanic youth. Tarrant County College knew their district, one of the largest and fastest growing in Texas, could play an important role in breaking down that barrier.

When we first met, TCC already had four healthy campuses which served primarily suburban communities. They wanted a new downtown campus that would provide access for the underserved. There would be two immediate bonuses: Moving their nursing and allied health programs to a downtown campus would bring those programs closer to existing hospitals and at the same time, people already working downtown could now enroll in TCC's vibrant continuing education program. Here was another chance to leverage public work for the community's greater benefit.

Because Fort Worth sits on a bluff, you literally can't see the Trinity River until you get to the edge. Like many North American cities, it has historically turned its back to the river. In fact, when we first arrived and walked around the city that evening, the people we met in the street couldn't even point to where the river was! So when we set out to design the new campus, one of the things we really wanted to do was to link the downtown to its forgotten waterfront. By using the new campus to carve a pathway through the bluff, down to the river, we've been able to create a visual and physical link to the downtown. A dynamic series of campus buildings on either side of a central pathway descend down to the water through a series of courtyards and walkways. The campus grade is on an accessible 5 percent slope, so there's no need for wheelchair ramps. These buildings are scaled and arranged in such a way that they have become an extension of the city's downtown street system, right to the river.

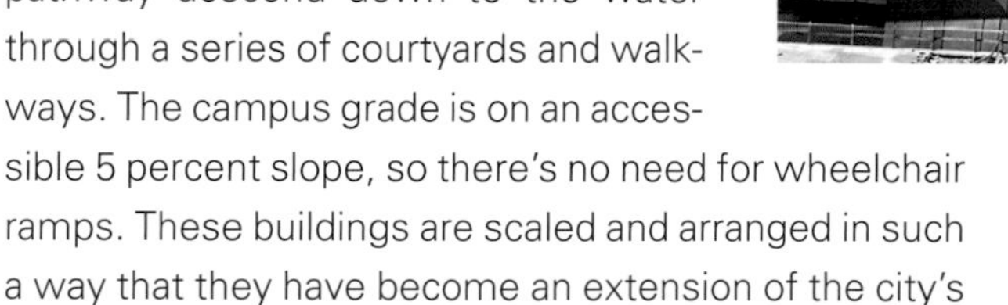

One of the really big differences between Vancouver and Fort Worth is climate. It gets tremendously hot in Fort Worth. In the hottest months, when temperatures routinely break 100°F (37.5°C), it seems virtually impossible to spend any extended time outside. At least we thought so, until we had the good fortune to dine at an outdoor Mexican restaurant in town called Joe T. Garcia's, a hugely popular Fort Worth restaurant that is almost entirely outdoors. The restaurant has a series of courtyards which are naturally cooled through the

Site plan

judicious use of planting, shade, and water features. Like other regular customers, we soon found that as long as you're in the shade, and particularly if you are near water, it's remarkably pleasant outside, even in the summer. So why not extend the downtown campus's outdoor "temperate" season for students and teachers by fostering microclimates using prevailing wind, shade, plantings, and water?

Typically, Forth Worth's major buildings are designed with big, air-conditioned interior lobbies and corridors. Instead, we designed a series of narrow buildings, easily lit with daylight, and accessible from these temperate courtyards and galleries. The result is that these lobbies and corridors are no longer needed. Instead, you're generally walking through outdoor shaded spaces. While actually building less, we've provided lots of space and opportunity for informal outdoor gatherings and interaction. That's the ultimate in sustainability: not having to make as much building in the first place.

Our original design was for the campus to span across the Trinity River. This gave the campus a significant presence downtown, but would allow it to expand onto more available land uptown, north of the river. Construction was already underway on the downtown campus buildings when the TCCD had a unique opportunity to purchase a large nearby building downtown for an extremely reasonable price. As a result, the proposed uptown site was no longer required. Although only the downtown side of our plan for TCC's new campus (now christened the Trinity East Campus) was implemented, we are pleased that Fort Worth will at least have a large college population downtown as well as a strong public connection to the waterfront, as already evident in these construction photographs. And like TCC, we're hopeful that architecture has played a role in bootstrap social change for the downtown community. And in ten years, who knows?

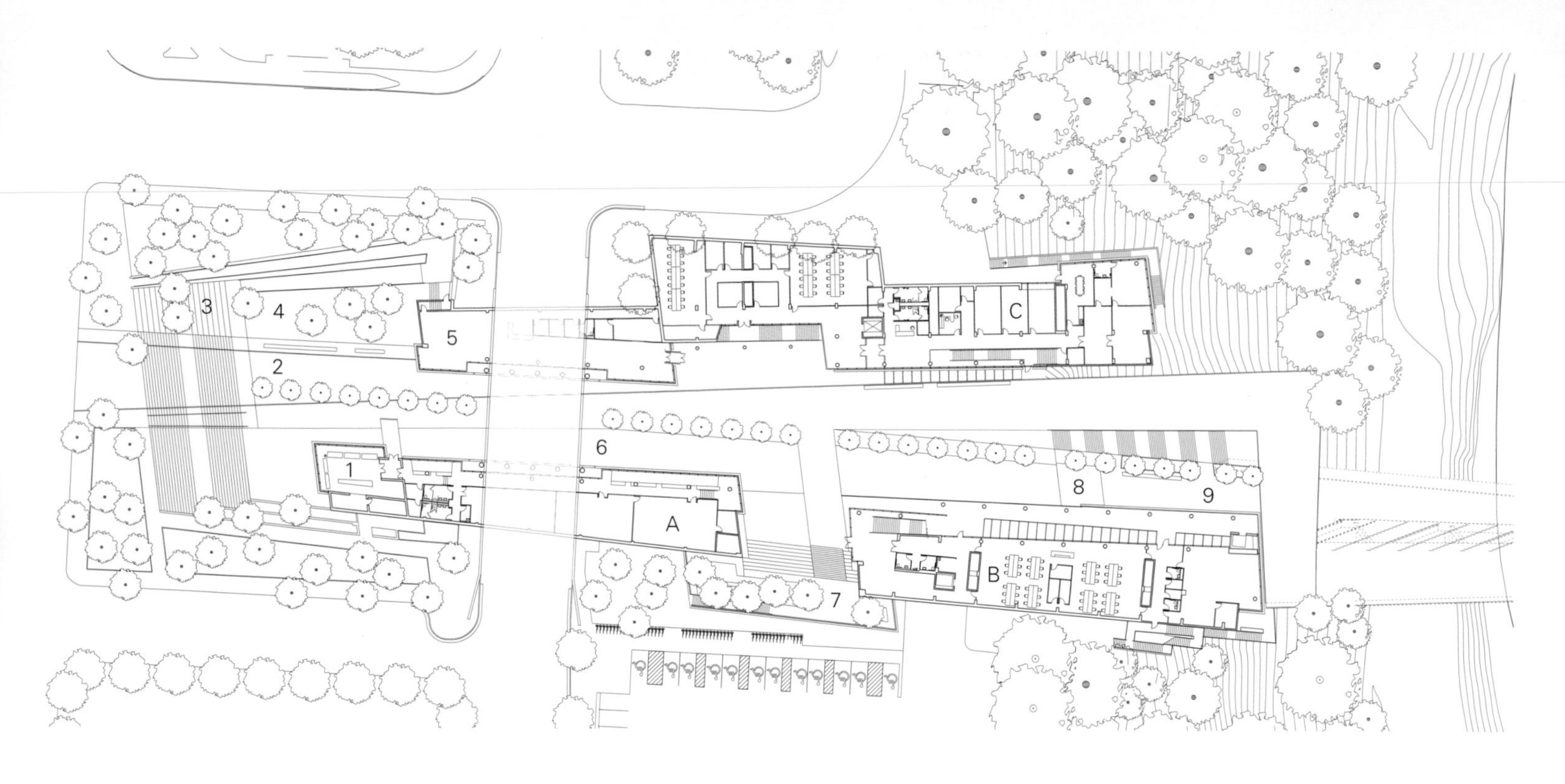

Downtown Campus Plan

0 10 25 50

A: labs, classrooms, offices
B: auditoriums, classrooms, offices, conference rooms
C: labs, classrooms

1. Welcome center
2. Plaza
3. Outdoor seating area
4. Stage lawn
5. Bookstore
6. Fountain
7. Upper courtyard
8. Waterfall
9. Lower courtyard

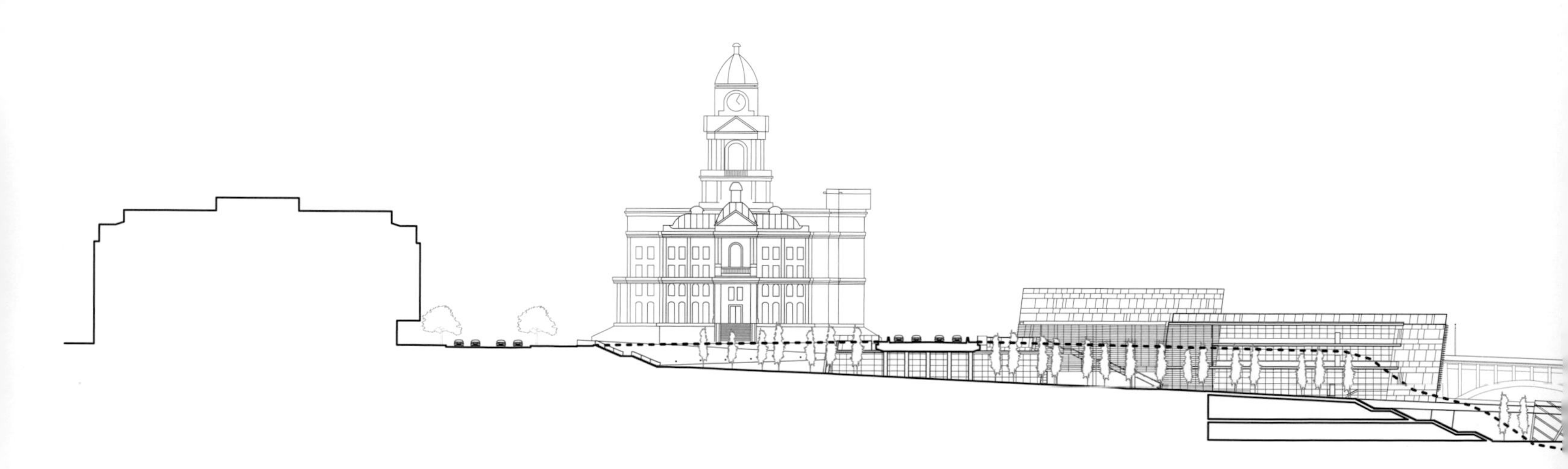

Site section

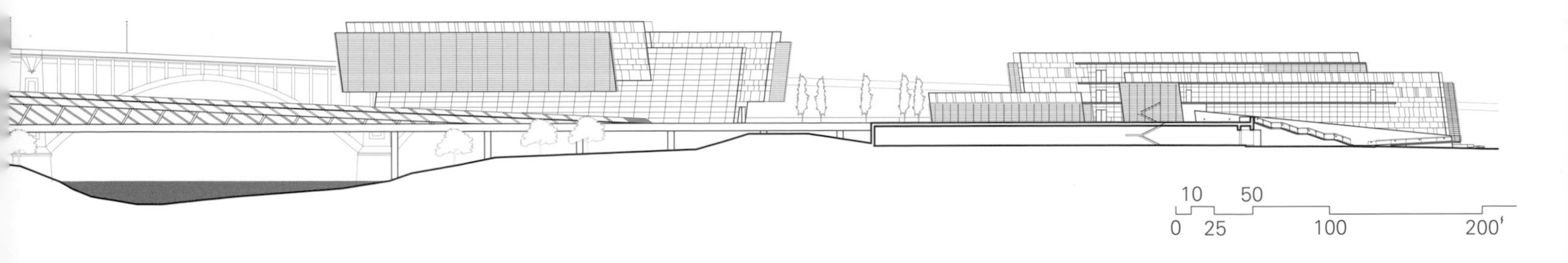
10
50
0
25
100
200'

Canada Pavilion

How do you say "Canada" in a few seconds? World expositions are all about first impressions so that was our challenge in designing the Canada Pavilion for Expo '92 in Seville, Spain. Most international pavilions are packed full of stuff that countries are trying to show off, but in our pavilion we wanted to represent the vastness of Canada. When you walked in there was nothing—just space: a very cool space. It was widely considered Expo '92's most popular international pavilion. The Spanish press, paraphrasing Gulf War jargon of the day, headlined photos of the outrageous queues as "the mother of all lineups." It was the first of the international pavilions to break ground, the first to be completed, and one of few international pavilions that the Spanish kept as legacy buildings. Here's how we accomplished it.

It didn't seem appropriate to parachute a Canadian building into Spain. Instead, we decided to interpret Spanish architecture as Canadians. So the building components reflected Spain: tiles, water, colonnades, and courtyards, but they were designed and built with Canadian characteristics. Our tiles were massive and made of zinc rather than ceramic; and where Spanish fountains throw water into the air, our courtyard wall of water flowed down smoothly, like Canada's many rivers and waterfalls.

Why zinc walls? Well, we actually started out thinking wood for the exterior of the building, but we couldn't find any industry support. We knew Canada was (and still is) the world's largest producer of zinc, and we thought it could be an intriguing material. Europeans have been using zinc on their roofs for centuries, but before Expo '92 no one had used it as a wall cladding. As a result of our pavilion, zinc wall cladding is now a multimillion dollar business.

We decided to build a colonnade on two sides through which people could enter the pavilion at any point. By raising the pavilion's main attraction, the box-like IMAX theatre, up on stilts, we now had some extra space underneath it for an entry courtyard and amphitheater. This area was naturally cooled by both a waterfall and ventilation through the colonnade—the way traditional Spanish houses with courtyards handle the heat. Because it was almost 18°F (10°C) cooler than Spain's stifling summer heat, people thought this space was mechanically air-conditioned, even though it was entirely natural.

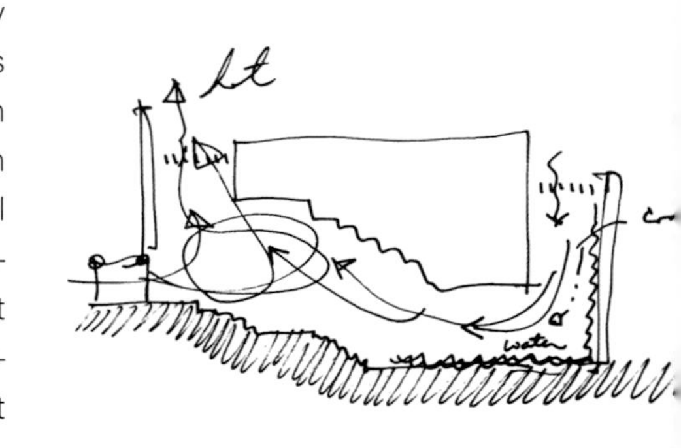

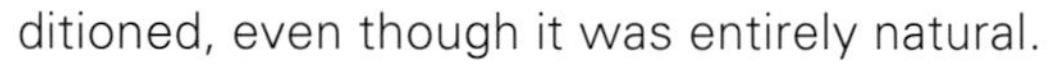

This courtyard became a magical oasis thanks to our collaboration with some remarkable Vancouver artists and craftsmen. At the time, Canadians were the world leaders in holographic technology, and we showcased this by installing a holographic diffraction grating and mirrors on the back wall of the courtyard. When water ran over this wall, it reflected the diffracted light, creating immense spatial depth that changed color depending on the particular light source and viewing angle. Each visitor literally changed their own experience as they moved around. And the mirrors replicated all of this, creating a sense of infinity. It was like looking at the vast play of Canada's northern lights.

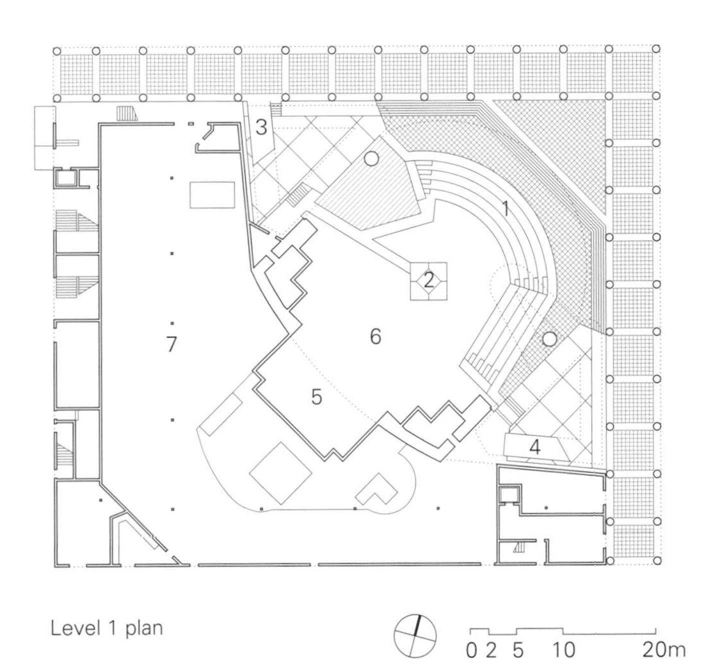

Level 1 plan

0 2 5 10 20m

1. Performance hall
2. Stage
3. Entrance ramp
4. Exit ramp
5. Light well
6. Pool
7. Exhibition space

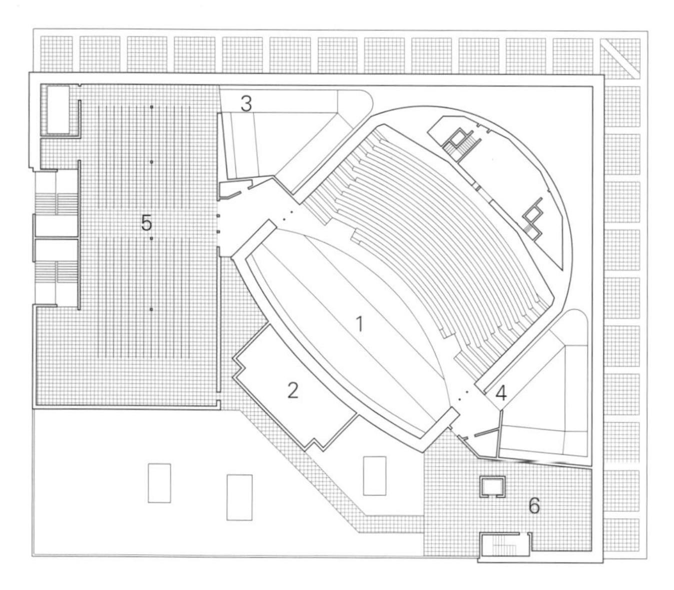

Level 3 plan

1. IMAX theater
2. Light well
3. Entrance ramp
4. Exit ramp
5. Mezzanine
6. VIP waiting lounge

CANADA

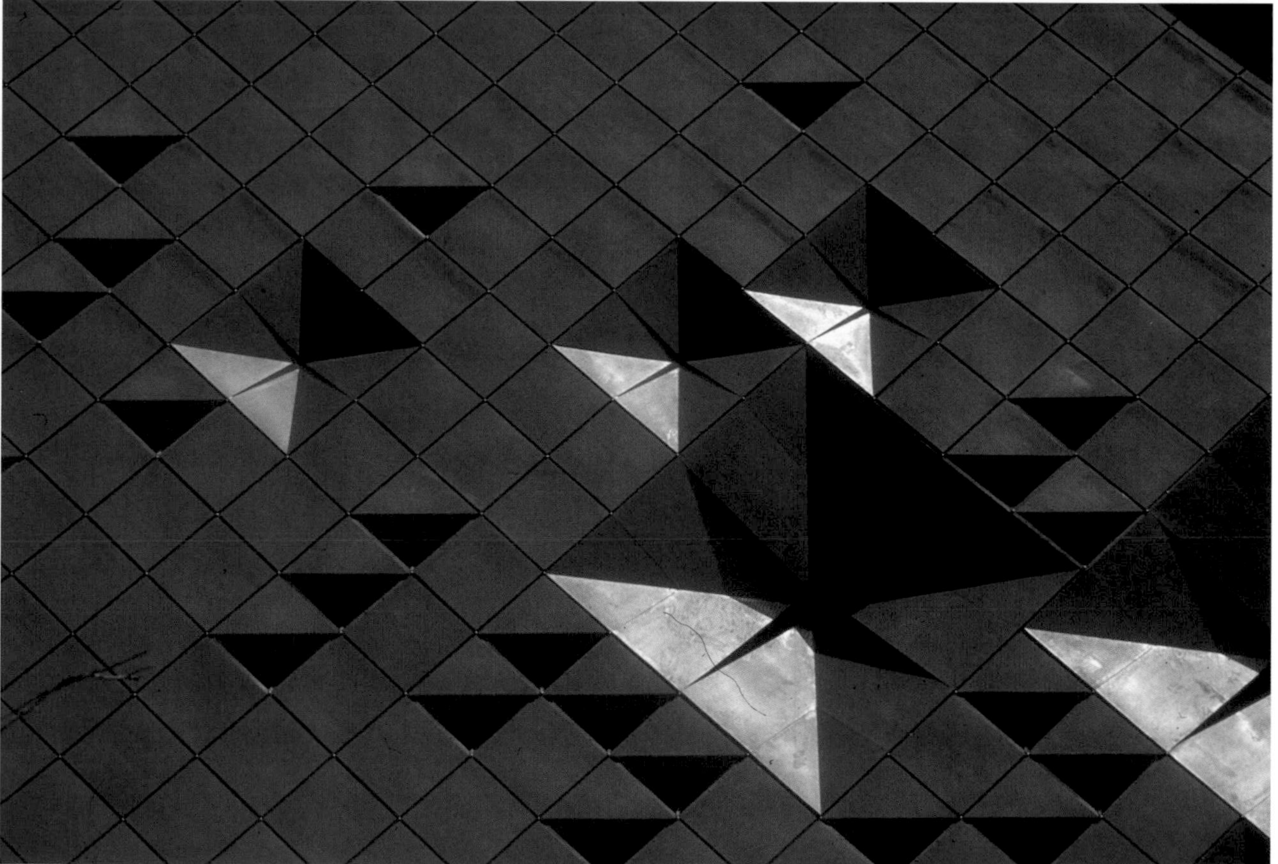

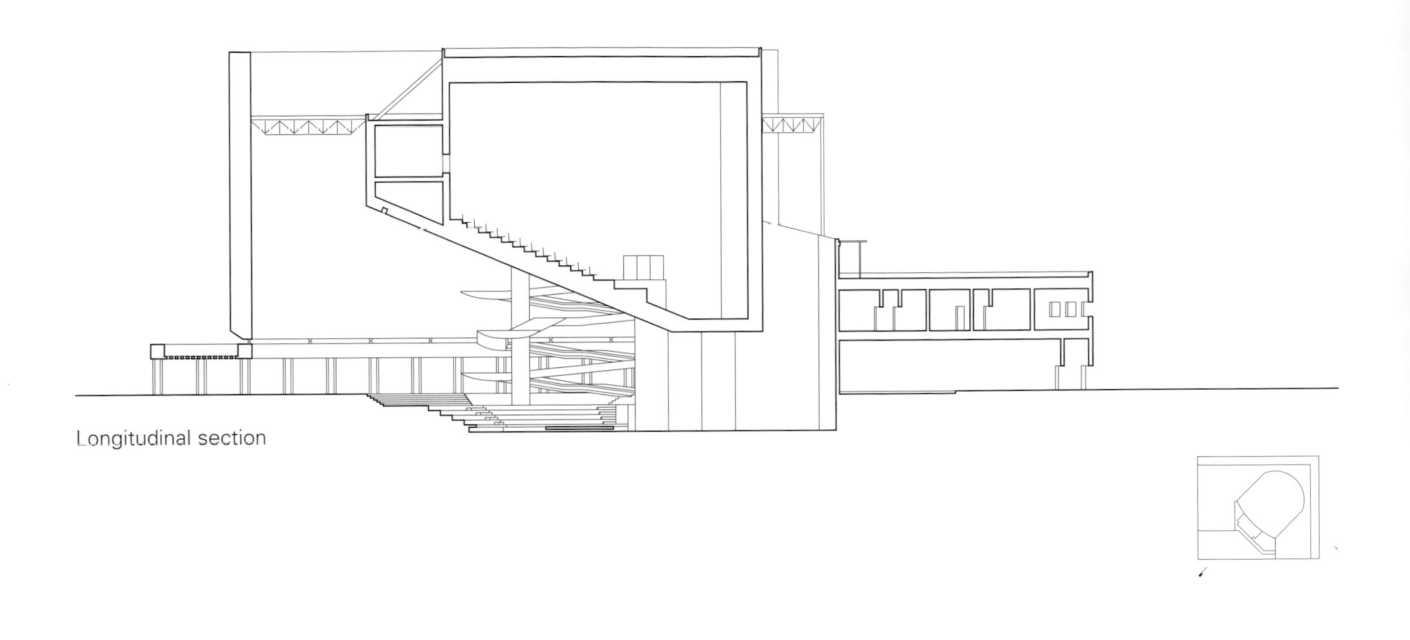

Longitudinal section

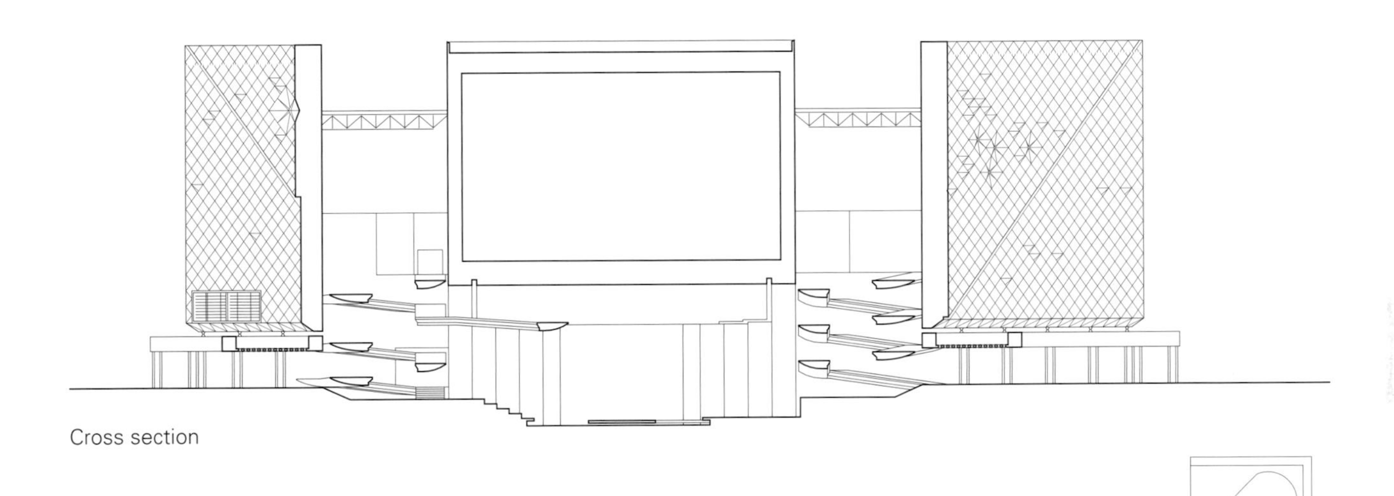

Cross section

0 2 5 10 20m

CANADA

Acadia Residence

These were wonderful clients. We'd never met them before they came to our office, but they clearly had done their research, and had already seen most of the buildings we have designed in Vancouver. We only occasionally do houses, and when we said it could take a year and a half just to design because we needed to fit it in among our larger project commitments, they said that was fine, they would wait. When we asked, "What do you need?" They simply said, "Three bedrooms. The rest is up to you."

For us, small projects like houses are really important because they are laboratories to develop ideas that we can then apply to our larger projects. They also provide an opportunity for Bing to work very directly on a project himself, and to train promising members of our junior staff.

It was a typical ninety-foot lot in a good Vancouver neighborhood, but the site was not particularly distinguished. There were certainly no real views, so to design the house we had to first design its setting. The house was really designed as a pavilion that looks out into five different gardens. We started by sitting down and asking, what are the garden views we want them to see? Every morning when this family gets up to have breakfast, they have a different view of nature.

Because they were a young couple from China, we drew inspiration from the beautiful private water gardens in Suzhou, famous for their serenity and distinct pagoda roofs. Finding mature planting material for the gardens was critical. Every weekend, Bing and his wife Bonnie would go to nurseries to choose each plant and tree so that we knew they would fit in.

When we were about to start construction, the owner asked, "If we had a little bit more money, what else would you do?" We proposed glass bridges in the center of the house, to bring light down into the lower floors. We also wanted to wrap the whole roof with zinc, inside and out. He said, "Let's do it!"

In many respects, the whole house was an R&D project. We used simple materials: glass, concrete, and steel, but we experimented with different ways of using them. It's actually a very humble house, with an understated exterior. The family really loves it and maintains it meticulously. Sometimes they'll phone and say, "You've got to come over and see the garden right now! It's so beautiful today."

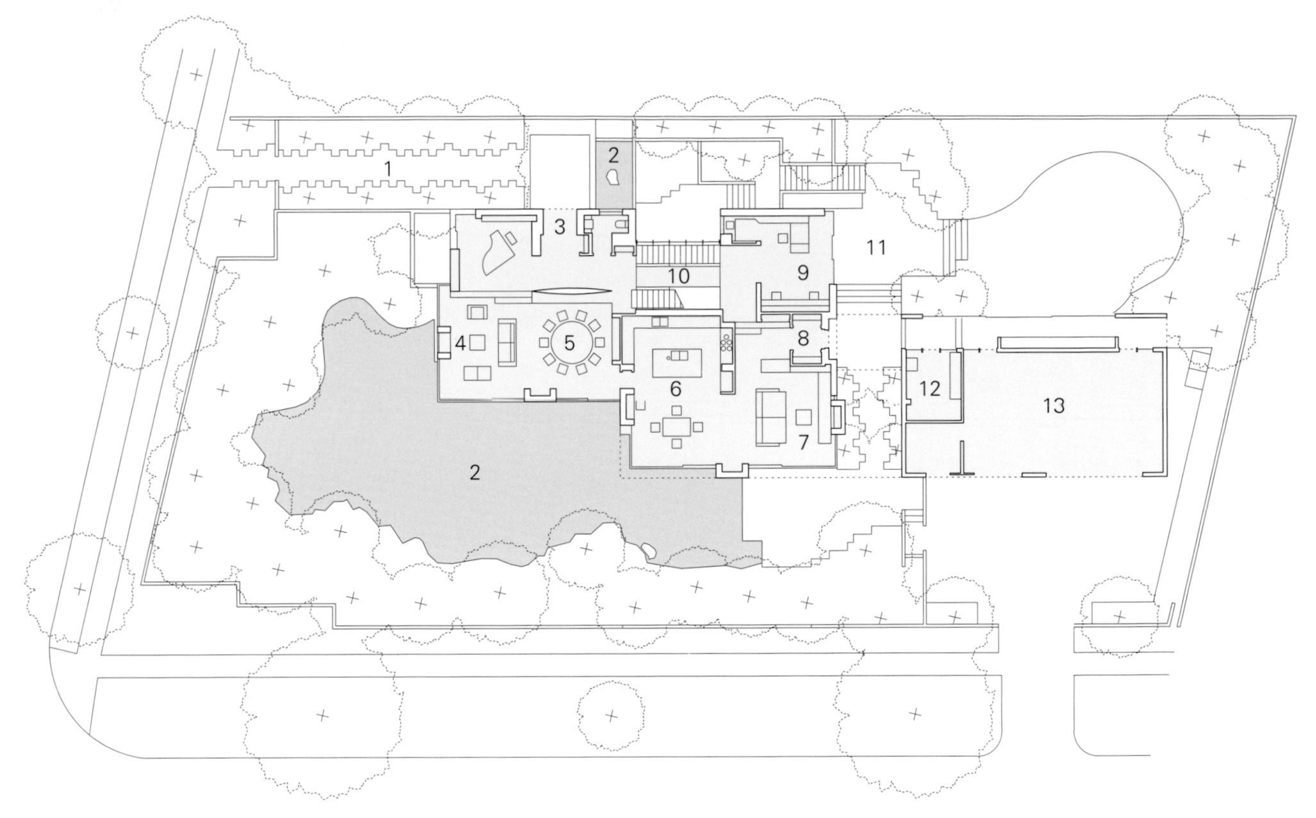

Ground level plan

1. Front entry court
2. Pond
3. Entry
4. Living room
5. Dining room
6. Kitchen
7. Family room
8. Rear entry
9. Studio
10. Glass bridge
11. Stone patio
12. Work room
13. Garage

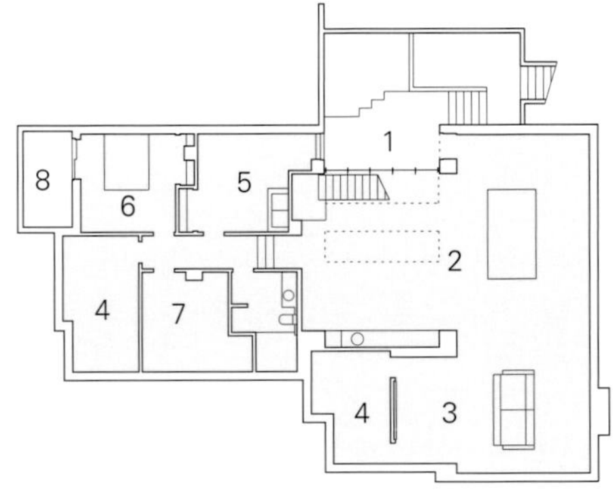

Basement plan

1. Courtyard
2. Recreation room
3. Home theater
4. Storage
5. Laundry
6. Guest bedroom
7. Mechanical
8. Light well

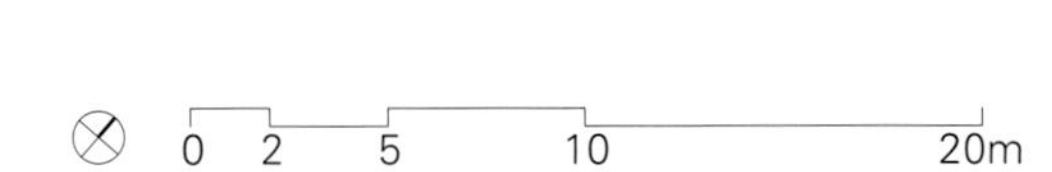

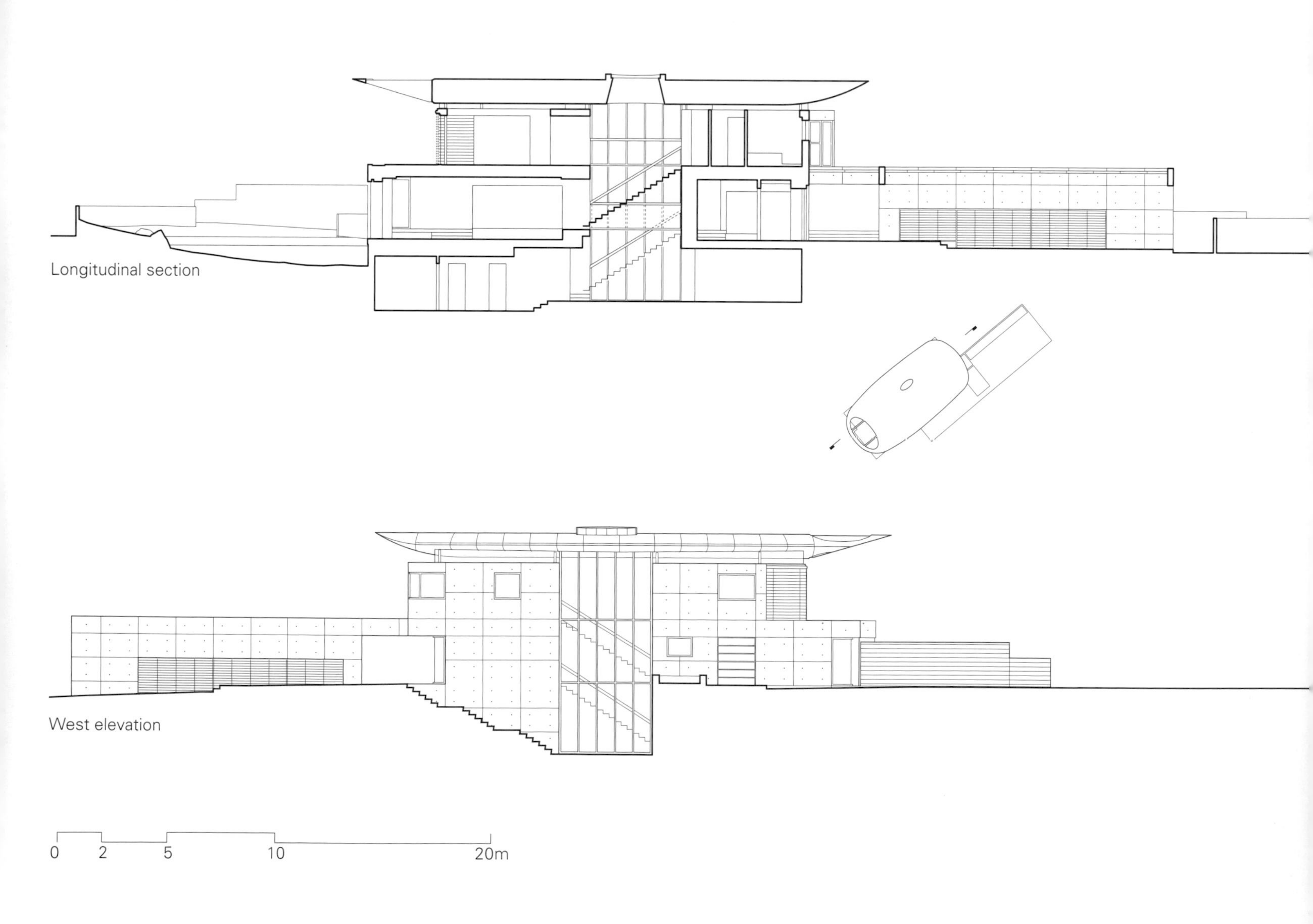

Longitudinal section

West elevation

Second floor plan

1. Glass bridge
2. Tatami room
3. Master bedroom
4. Bedroom
5. Roof terrace
6. Garage, below

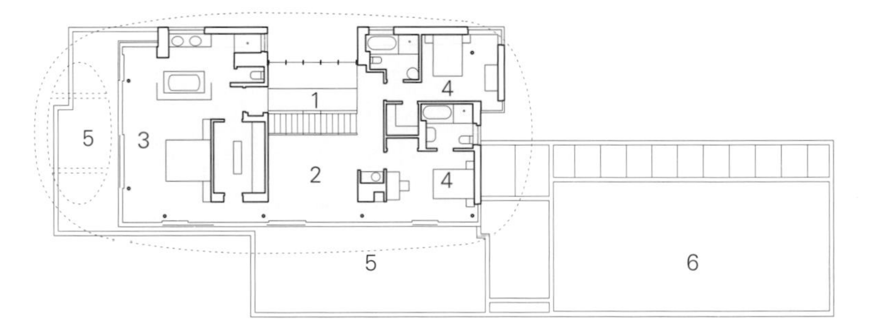

Selected Works

Randall School Development + Rubell Art Museum*
Washington, D.C., USA
2010–present
Historic site redevelopment/
Museum/Mixed-use

Tianjin Financial District Office Towers
Tianjin, China
2010–present
Mixed-use development complex/
Invited competition

Shui Wan Cun Towers
Shenzen, China
2009–present
Mixed-use development complex

Surrey City Centre Library*
Surrey, British Columbia, Canada
2009–2011
Municipal library

Private Residence
Calgary, Alberta, Canada
2008–present
Private residence

Arena Stage
Washington, D.C., USA
2001–2010
Historic site redevelopment/
Performing arts complex

Aberdeen Phase 3
Richmond, British Columbia, Canada
2006–present
Office and retail development

Surrey City Hall*
Surrey, British Columbia, Canada
2007–2009
Planning proposal

Tantalus Winery*
Kelowna, British Columbia, Canada
2007–2009
Winery development proposal

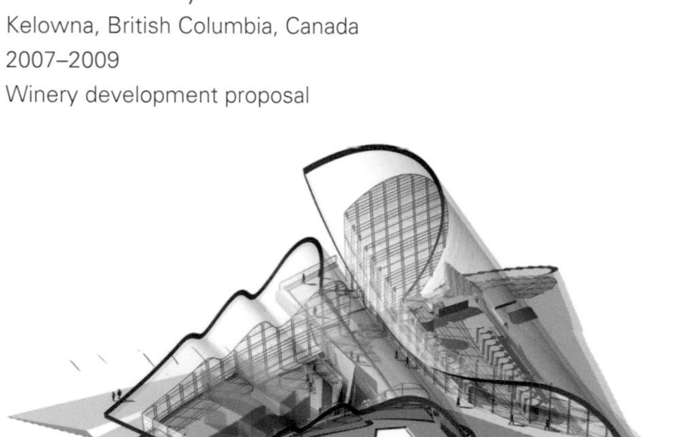

Harwood Condominiums and Heritage House
Vancouver, British Columbia, Canada
2005–present
Residential development

Tarrant County College
Fort Worth, Texas, USA
2004–present
Campus buildings/Master plan

Whistler 2010 Legacy Plaza
Whistler, British Columbia, Canada
2007–2010
Olympic medals venue concept

Sunalta Redevelopment Plan
Calgary, Alberta, Canada
2008–2009
Urban master plan

SAIT Polytechnic Parking Structure
Calgary, Alberta, Canada
2008–2009
Multi-level parking structure

Festival of Architecture*
London, England
2008
Public installation

BC-Canada House Olympic Venue
Beijing, China
2008
Entry feature

SAIT Polytechnic Campus
Calgary, Alberta, Canada
2006–2008
Campus master plan

Fort Worth Bridges*
Fort Worth, Texas, USA
2007
Urban infrastructure concept

Sunset Community Centre
Vancouver, British Columbia, Canada
2004–2007
Community centre

Aberdeen Phase 2
Richmond, British Colubmia, Canada
2002–2007
Residential development

Crow Creek Bridge*
Tulsa, Oklahoma, USA
2006
Urban infrastructure concept

Tulsa Waterfront Development Plan
Tulsa, Oklahoma, USA
2005–2006
Master plan

Trinity Uptown Plan
Fort Worth, Texas, USA
2004–2006
Master plan

Acadia Residence
Vancouver, British Columbia, Canada
2002–2004
Private residence

Shanghai Expo 2010 Master Plan*
Shanghai, China
2004
Invited competition

National Association of Realtors Office
Washington, D.C., USA
2004
Invited competition

Georgia Hotel Tower*
Vancouver, British Columbia, Canada
2002
Historic building/Hotel development proposal

Aberdeen Phase 1
Richmond, British Columbia, Canada
1999–2004
Commercial retail development

Central City / Simon Fraser University
Surrey, British Columbia, Canada
1999–2004
Office/Retail/Academic complex

788 Richards
Vancouver, British Columbia, Canada
2003
Mixed-use development proposal

Janacek Concert Hall*
Brno, Czech Republic
2003
Invited competition

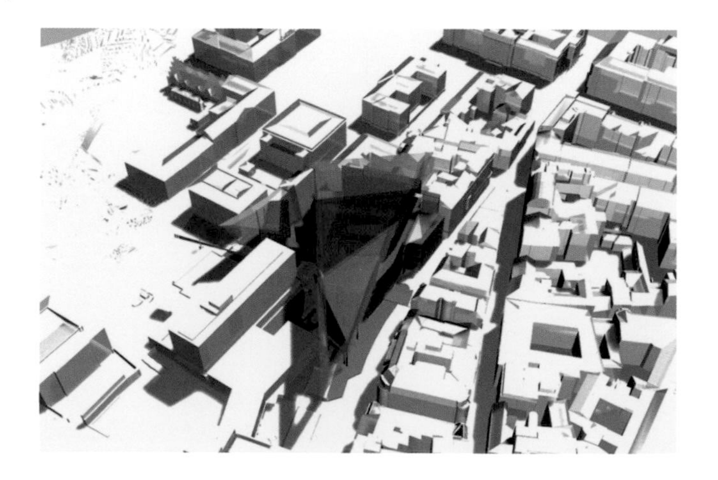

Anacostia Waterfront Initiative
Washington, D.C., USA
2003
Waterfront master plan

Royal Ontario Museum Expansion*
Toronto, Ontario, Canada
2001–2002
Invited competition

Yuxi Concert Hall*
Yuxi, China
2000–2002
Performance theater concept

Yuxi and Dayingjie Town Centre Master Plan
Yuxi, China
2000
Master plan

Arts Club Theatre
Vancouver, British Columbia, Canada
2000
Performance theater concept

Nike Research Campus
Surrey, British Columbia, Canada
1998
Industrial complex master plan concept

Vancouver Aquarium Expansion*
Vancouver, British Columbia, Canada
1997–1999
Themed attraction expansion

Victoria Inner Harbour Study
Victoria, British Columbia, Canada
1998
Master plan

Saskatoon Waterfront Study
Saskatoon, Saskatchewan, Canada
1997–1998
Master plan

Surrey Performing Arts
Surrey, British Columbia, Canada
1996–1998
Programming/Master plan

Hong Kong '97 Expo
Hong Kong, China
1996–1997
Waterfront master plan concept

BC Place Convention Centre
Vancouver, British Columbia, Canada
1995
MIxed-use redevelopment concept

Pointe Tower*
Vancouver, British Columbia, Canada
1993–1997
Residential Complex

Chan Centre for the
Performing Arts
Vancouver, British Columbia, Canada
1992–1997
Concert Hall/Studio Theatre/
Cinema

Sun Sui Wah Restaurant
Vancouver, British Columbia, Canada
1993–1996
Restaurant and retail development

Downtown Convention
Centre
Vancouver, British Columbia, Canada
1994
Mixed-use complex/Invited
competition

Mayfair Lakes Golf
Clubhouse Expansion
Vancouver, British Columbia,
Canada
1991–1995
Recreation

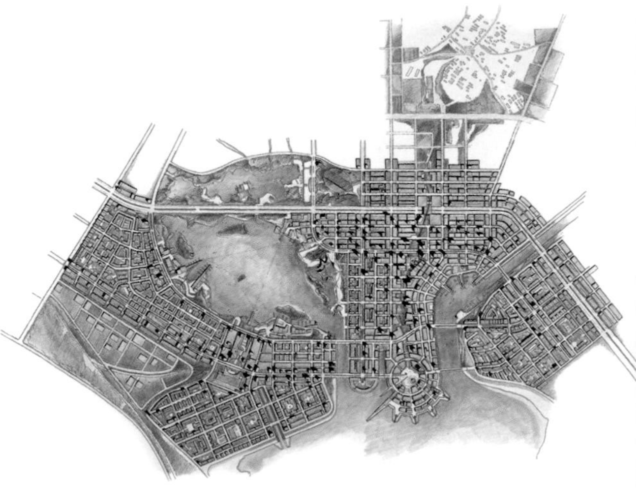

Dalian New Town
Master Plan*
Dalian, China
1993–1994
Invited competition

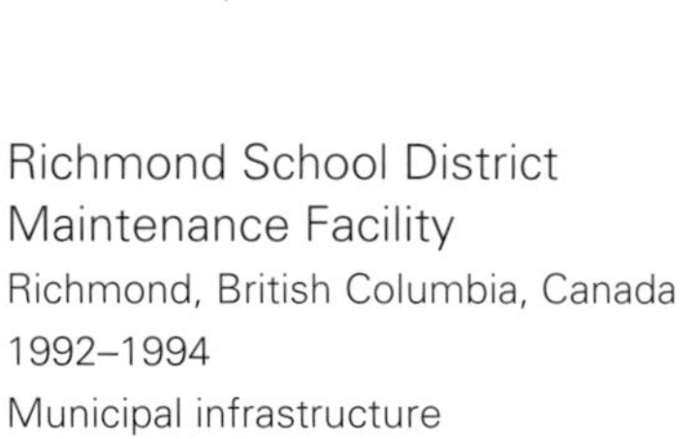

Richmond School District
Maintenance Facility
Richmond, British Columbia, Canada
1992–1994
Municipal infrastructure

Dynasty Restaurant
Vancouver, British Columbia, Canada
1993
Restaurant

Richmond McKinney
Elementary School
Vancouver, British Columbia, Canada
1992–1993
Public school

Chili Club Restaurant
Vancouver, British Columbia, Canada
1992–1993
Restaurant

1550 West 15th Tower
Vancouver, British Columbia, Canada
1990–1993
Residential tower

Canada Pavilion, Expo 92
Seville, Spain
1989–1992
Exposition venue

Point Grey Condo*
Vancouver, British Columbia, Canada
1984–1988
Residential development

855/899 Homer Tower*
Vancouver, British Columbia, Canada
1993
Office/Residential tower

938 Howe
Vancouver, British Columbia, Canada
1981-1991
Office tower

New World Harbourside Hotel
Vancouver, British Columbia, Canada
1988–1990
Renovation/Redevelopment

False Creek Yacht Club*
Vancouver, British Columbia, Canada
1989
Waterfront development

Northwest Territories Pavilion, Expo 86*
Vancouver, British Columbia, Canada
1985–1986
Exposition venue

Hong Kong Pavilion, Expo '86
Vancouver, British Columbia, Canada
1985–1986
Exposition venue/Open competition

Private Residence
Vancouver, British Columbia, Canada
1984
Single-family house

BTA Offices
Vancouver, British Columbia, Canada
1982
Office building

Awards

2010
2010 RAIC Firm of the Year, Royal Architectural Institute of Canada

2009
Award for Excellence in Achievement, Tilt-up Concrete Association (Sunset Community Centre, Vancouver, BC)

2008
Awards for Excellence in Concrete Construction, Grand CONNIE Award (Sunset Community Centre, Vancouver, BC)

Awards for Excellence in Concrete Construction, Tilt-up Structures (Sunset Community Centre, Vancouver, BC)

2007
Lieutenant-Governor of British Columbia Certificate of Merit for Excellence in Architecture, AIBC (Aberdeen Centre, Richmond, BC)

CLIDE Award, Center of Development Excellence (Trinity Uptown Plan, Fort Worth, TX)

2006
Western Living Residential Design Awards, Winner of Large Home Category (Acadia Street Residence, Vancouver, BC)

Awards for Excellence in Concrete Construction, Architectural Concrete (Acadia Street Residence, Vancouver, BC)

2005
Excellence on the Waterfront Awards - Top Honor, The Waterfront Center, Washington, D.C. (The Trinity Uptown Plan, Fort Worth, TX)

Merit Awards, Landscape Analysis & Planning, Boston Society of Landscape Architects (The Trinity Uptown Plan, Fort Worth, TX)

Citation Award, Wood Design Awards (Surrey Central City, Surrey, BC)

2004
Award of Excellence, Vancouver Regional Construction Association (Aberdeen Mall, Richmond, BC)

Illuminating Engineering Society & International Illumination Lighting Design Awards (Surrey Central City, Surrey, BC)

Marche International des Professionels de l'Immobilier (Cannes, France) Special Jury Prize (Surrey Central City, Surrey, BC)

Lieutenant-Governor of British Columbia Medal in Architecture, AIBC (Surrey Central City, Surrey, BC)

Architectural Institute of British Columbia Innovation Award (Surrey Central City, Surrey, BC)

PNW Region, Guth Award, Advanced to IIDA International Level (Surrey Central City, Surrey, BC)

PNW Region Waterbury Award for Lighting (Surrey Central City, Surrey, BC)

2002
Golden Jubilee Award

2001
CIP Award for Planning Excellence, Canadian Institute of Planners (Conceptual Development Plan for the City Center of Yuxi, China)

2000
Lieutenant-Governor of British Columbia Medal, AIBC (Pacific Canada Pavilion, Vancouver Aquarium, Vancouver, BC)

Architectural Institute of British Columbia Innovation Award (Pacific Canada Pavilion, Vancouver Aquarium, Vancouver, BC)

CRSI Design Award, Concrete Reinforcing Steel Institute (Chan Centre for the Performing Arts, Vancouver, BC)

1998
Lieutenant-Governor of British Columbia Medal, AIBC (Chan Centre for the Performing Arts, Vancouver, BC)

USITT Merit Award, United States Institute for Theater Technology (Chan Centre for the Performing Arts, Vancouver, BC)

1997
Winner, BC Steel Design Awards (Chan Centre for the Performing Arts, Vancouver, BC)

USITT Award, United States Institute for Theatre Technology (Chan Centre for the Performing Arts, Vancouver, BC)

Winner, Gold Georgie Award – Best Multi-Family Development (The Pointe, Residential Highrise Development, Vancouver, BC)

Winner, Silver Georgie Award – Best High-Rise Multi-Family Development (The Pointe, Residential Highrise Development, Vancouver, BC)

1995
Order of Canada

1994
Winner, Silver Georgie Award (889 Homer, Residential Highrise Development, Vancouver, BC)

1992
Lieutenant-Governor of British Columbia Medal, AIBC (False Creek Yacht Club/Anderson's Restaurant, Vancouver, BC)

1990
Governor General Medal, Royal Architectural Institute of Canada (Point Grey Road Condominiums, Vancouver, BC)

Governor General Medal, Royal Architectural Institute of Canada (False Creek Yacht Club/Anderson's Restaurant, Vancouver, BC)

Excellence on the Waterfront Award, The Waterfront Center, Washington, D.C. (False Creek Yacht Club / Anderson's Restaurant, Vancouver, BC)

1989
Winner, Canadian National Selection (Canada Pavilion, Expo '92, Seville, Spain)

American Hotel/Motel and Restaurant Gold Key Award (New World Harbourside Hotel, Dynasty Restaurant, Vancouver, BC)

Interior Designer's Institute of British Columbia Award (New World Harbourside Hotel, Dynasty Restaurant, Vancouver, BC)

1986
Canadian Travel and Tourism Award (Northwest Territories Pavilion, Expo '86, Vancouver, BC)

Canadian Wood Council Award (Northwest Territories Pavilion, Expo '86, Vancouver, BC)

1981
Canadian Architect Design Award (12th Avenue Condominiums, Vancouver, BC)

Selected Publications

2010

Beaver, Robyn. *21st Century Houses: 150 of the World's Best.* Mulgrave, Victoria: Images Publishing, 2010.

Bernstein, Fred A. "Washington's Fresh Coat of Greasepaint." *New York Times*, October 6, 2010.

Ingold, David. "Bing Thom's Arena Stage Expansion." *buildipedia.com*, April 21, 2010.

Kennicott, Philip. "Arena Stage's new building: a brilliant addition, and a challenge, to the city." *Washington Post*, September 26, 2010.

———. "Raising the Curtain on Bing Thom." *Washington Post*, September 26, 2010.

Macdonald, Christopher. *A Guidebook to Contemporary Architecture in Vancouver.* Vancouver: Douglas & McIntyre, 2010.

Marks, Peter. "Remodeled Arena Stage may transform D.C. theater and the city." *Washington Post*, September 26, 2010.

Murphy, Kim. "Vancouver engineers its own urban dream." *Los Angeles Times*, January 12, 2010.

Smith, Charlie. "How global warming might transform Vancouver's shoreline." *Georgia Straight* (Vancouver), March 18, 2010.

Stathaki, Ellie. "Retaking the Stage." *Wallpaper*, October 2010.

2009

Jones, Will. *Unbuilt Masterworks of the 21st Century.* London: Thames & Hudson, 2009.

Regan, Keith. "History with a cutting edge." *Achieving Business Excellence*, January 2009.

2008

"BC wood-wall marvel to loom over London's Trafalgar Square." *The Province* (Vancouver), June 4, 2008.

"Bing Thom to Receive Honorary Degree from the University of British Columbia." *Canadian Architect*, May 12, 2008.

Boddy, Trevor. "A good fit with both site and community." *Globe and Mail* (Toronto), April 11, 2008.

Ditmars, Hadani. "The architecture of Vancouverism." *The Guardian*, June 27, 2008.

———. *Wallpaper City Guide: Vancouver.* New York: Phaidon Press, 2008.

———. "Will Vancouverism take root in downtown London?" *Globe and Mail*, June 25, 2008.

Harris, Michael. "The Bing Picture." *Vancouver Magazine*, June 2008.

Liang, Victor. "Blueprint of a Community." *Ricepaper* 13, no. 3.

Osbaldeston, Mark. *Unbuilt Toronto: A History of the City That Might Have Been.* Toronto: Dundum Press, 2008.

Pressley, Nelson. "Arena, the Detouring Theater Company." *Washington Post*, February 24, 2008.

Rochon, Lisa. "Straight from B.C., ideas as big as all Texas." *Globe and Mail* (Toronto), November 29, 2008.

"Vancouverism Transforms Trafalgar Square and maybe more?" *Hinge* 157 (August 2008).

"Vancouverism: Westcoast Architecture + City-Building exhibition unveiled in London, UK." *Canadian Architect*, June 24, 2008.

"West Coasting, Sunset Community Centre," *Hinge* 161 (December 2008).

2007

Baker, Max. "Trinity Uptown—On a New Path." *Fort Worth Star-Telegram*, January 26, 2007.

Boddy, Trevor. "A symphony of house and garden." *Globe and Mail* (Toronto), March 2, 2007.

Francis, Robert. "Bridging the Gap." *Fort Worth Business*, February 11, 2007.

Mosier, Jeff. "In FW, A Glimpse of Grandeur." *Dallas News*, January 26, 2007.

Rochon, Lisa. "Landmarks, pinnacles, passages." *Globe and Mail* (Toronto), December 29, 2007.

Tetley, Deborah. "SAIT Looks to Future." *Calgary Herald*, May 4, 2007.

2006

Barber, Brian. "Designer Goes With River's Flow." *Tulsa World*, July 23, 2006.

Gill, Alexandra. "Bing Thom's Vision for a New Vancouver." *Globe and Mail* (Toronto), May 13, 2006.

Lassek, P. J. "Plan Would Cut West Bank." *Tulsa World*, October 18, 2006.

McLellan, Wendy. "SFU Surrey Adds Gown to Town." *The Province* (Vancouver), August 31, 2006.

Roohani, Alexis. "A home designed from the garden in." *Globe and Mail* (Toronto), June 30, 2006.

Rule, Carolann. "Grand Illusion." *Western Living*, October 2006.

Taggart, Jim. "Suburban Shift." *Canadian Architect*, August 2006.

2005

Bernstein, Fred A. "Revitalizing the Banks of Washington's Forgotten River." *New York Times*, March 27, 2005.

Dunham-Jones, Ellen. "Suburban Retrofits, Demographics and Sustainability, Places." *Forum of Environmental Design* 17, no. 2.

Patterson, Jennifer. "Philosopher Bing." *Design Quarterly*, Winter 2005.

Slessor, Catherine. "Shiny Shopping." *Architectural Review*, November 2005.

"Surrey Central City." *Wood Design & Building*, Autumn 2005.

2004

Arnone, Michael. "The Malls of Acadame." *Chronicle of Higher Education*, October 29, 2004.

Baker, Sandra. "Plan for Campus Unveiled." *Fort Worth Star-Telegram*, October 30, 2004.

Boddy, Trevor. "East Meets West at Aberdeen," *Vancouver Sun*, January 19, 2004.

———. "Surrey Central City Wins 'Urban Development Oscar.'" *Vancouver Sun*, March 16, 2004.

Colley, Ted. "Central City Win's 'Oscar.'" *The Now* (Surrey), March 17, 2004.

"Come Machina Scenica—Arena Stage, Washington, DC." *L'ARCA*, 191, 2004.

Grdadolnik, Helena. "Master Builders." *Canadian Architect*, September 2004.

Hunter, Stuart. "Central City Wins 'Oscar.'" *The Province* (Vancouver), March 18, 2004.

Paganelli, Carlo. "Arena Stage, Washington." *L'ARCA* (April 2004).

Patterson, Jennifer. "2004 VRCA Awards of Excellence—Curved and Complex." *Construction Business*, November/December 2004.

Pressley, Nelson. "Creating Creative Spaces," *Washington Post*, December 12, 2004.

Schurman, Mitchell. "Designer Using His Flair on New TCC Campus." *Fort Worth Star-Telegram*, November 3, 2004.

Slessor, Catherine. "Touching Heaven." *Architectural Review*, March 2004.

Taggart, Jim, "Connect the Sprawl." *Canadian Architect*, March 2004.

Tinsley, M. Anna. "Model of Trinity River Vision Plan on Display." *Fort Worth Star-Telegram*, December 8, 2004.

Von Hahn, Karen. "Nouveau Richmond." *Globe and Mail*, January 10, 2004.

Wenjun, Zhi, and Cai Yu. "Factualism and Innovation: Bing Thom Architects and its Works." *Time & Architecture*, July 2004.

2003

"Bigger Theater for Washington." *New York Times*, September 29, 2003.

"Central Focus." *Architectural Review*, September 2003.

Forgey, Benjamin. "Standing Ovation." *Washington Post*, September 27, 2003.

Rochon, Lisa. "Thom Goes to Washington." *Globe and Mail* (Toronto), October 8, 2003.

Rossiter, Sean. "Vancouver's Designs Flatter the World." *The Vancouver Sun*, March 15, 2003.

2002

Haden, Bruce. "Sea Change." *Canadian Architect*, November, 2002.

Roan, Neill Archer. *Scale + Timbre: The Chan Centre for the Performing Arts*. London: Black Dog Publishing, 2002.

2001

"Chan Centre of UBC, Vancouver, Canada, 1998." *World Architecture*, October 2001.

2000

MacLellan, Lila. "Tidal Change." *Western Living*, April 2000.

Warson, Albert. "TechBC Campus Meets the Mall." *Globe and Mail* (Toronto), October 3, 2000.

1998

Dritmanis, John. "The Chan Centre In Concert." *Western Living*, September 1998.

Haden, Bruce. "Concert Halls 1: Pacific Opus." *Canadian Architect*, March 1998.

Weder, Adele. "On the Verge—Bing Thom Architects." *Azure*, January/February 1998.

1997

Abell, Tia. "Chan Centre: Illusion of Enchantment." *Pacific Rim*, 1997.

1992

"Spanish Design, the Canadian Way." *Architectural Record*, November 1992.

1991

McPhedran, Kerry. "Los Tres Caballeros." *Canadian Architect*, October 1991.

1990

Dubois, Macy. "Going to the Fair." *Canadian Architect*, October 1990.

"Betonperle Mit Gläserner Schale." *Häuser*, February 1990.

"Vancouver: Yacht Club Ohne Seefahrt—Romantik." *Häuser*, January 1990.

SPRINKLER SYSTEM

Acknowledgments

Writing:
Kerry McPhedran
Michael Heeney

The Architecture:
Our buildings are the product of a rich collaboration between our many colleagues here at Bing Thom Architects and the numerous clients, consultants, and craftsmen that make our work possible. We are indebted to them all.

In particular, the work illustrated in this book would not have been possible without the creativity, talent, and hard work of the numerous staff who have worked with us over the past twenty-eight years. Regrettably, it has proven impossible to assemble a comprehensive list; however, we want to acknowledge that each one has made a significant contribution and are part of our success. We want to single out the current senior management team who are so critical to our success, and whose talent will lead the firm far into the future:

James Brown
John Camfield
Shinobu Homma
Venelin Kokalov
Ling Meng
Helen Ritts
Francis Yan

Bing Thom Architects Inc.
1430 Burrard Street
Vancouver, BC
Canada, V6Z 2A3
604 682-1881
office@bingthomarchitects.com
www.bingthomarchitects.com

Photography Credits

All images are property of Bing Thom Architects unless otherwise credited.

Nic Lehoux: Cover, 2–3, 6–7, 10–11, 14–15, 18–19, 22–23, 24–25, 26–27, 28–29, 30–31, 32, 34–35, 36–37, 38–39, 40–41, 44–45, 46–47, 48–49, 50–51, 52–53, 54–55, 56, 64 (bottom), 66, 71 (top), 74, 81, 82–83, 85, 86, 88–89, 90–91, 94–95, 96–97, 99, 100–101, 102–103, 104 (top), 105, 107, 108–109, 110–111, 112–113, 114–115, 116–117, 118–119, 120–121, 122–123, 124–125, 126–127, 128 (top/bottom), 129, 130, 132–133, 134–135, 136–137, 138–139, 140 (middle/bottom), 141, 142, 144–145, 146, 148–149, 152–153, 155, 156–157, 158–159, 161, 162–163, 175, 176, 178–179, 180–181, 182–183, 184–185, 186–187, 188–189, 190–191, 198–199, 202–203, 206–207

Balthazar Korab: 21

Horst Thanhäuser: 57 (bottom), 60 (top), 76 (top), 164–165, 166–167, 168–169, 170, 172–173, 197 (bottom)

Wayne Thom: 58 (top), 64 (top), 196 (top/bottom)

Simon Scott: 58 (bottom), 194 (top), 197 (middle)

Frank Mayrs: 59, 67, 197 (top)

Martin Tessler: 60 (bottom), 62–63, 71 (bottom), 84, 92–93, 98, 195 (top/middle right)

Peter Andersen: 69 (top)

Collin Goldie: 79 (bottom), 192 (upper left/bottom left), 193 (upper/lower right), 194 (bottom)

Mark Sheldrick: 140 (top)

Morley von Sternberg: 193 (bottom left)